Sacagawea

written by **Joeming Dunn**
illustrated by **Rod Espinosa**

magic
wagon

visit us at
www.abdopublishing.com

Published by Magic Wagon, a division of the ABDO Publishing Group, 8000 West 78th Street, Edina, Minnesota 55439. Copyright © 2009 by Abdo Consulting Group, Inc. International copyrights reserved in all countries. All rights reserved. No part of this book may be reproduced in any form without written permission from the publisher.
Graphic Planet™ is a trademark and logo of Magic Wagon.

Printed in the United States.

Written by Joeming Dunn
Illustrated by Rod Espinosa
Edited by Stephanie Hedlund and Rochelle Baltzer
Interior layout and design by Antarctic Press
Cover art by Rod Espinosa
Cover design by Neil Klinepier

Library of Congress Cataloging-in-Publication Data

Dunn, Joeming W.
   Sacagawea / written by Joeming Dunn ; illustrated by Rod Espinosa.
     p. cm. -- (Bio-graphics)
   Includes bibliographical references and index.
   ISBN 978-1-60270-176-2 (alk. paper)
   1. Sacagawea--Juvenile literature. 2. Shoshoni women--Biography--Juvenile literature. 3. Shoshoni Indians--Biography--Juvenile literature. 4. Lewis and Clark Expedition (1804-1806)--Juvenile literature. I. Espinosa, Rod, ill. II. Title.

F592.7.S123D86 2009
978.004'9745740092--dc22
[B]   2007051514

TABLE of CONTENTS

Timeline

1788 – Sacagawea was believed to have been born in present-day Idaho.

1800 – Sacagawea was kidnapped by a Hidatsa tribe.

1804 – Toussaint Charbonneau bought Sacagawea and made her his wife.

1805 – Sacagawea joined the Lewis and Clark Expedition as an interpreter with her husband.

1806 – The Corps of Discovery returned to the Hidatsa village, where Sacagawea and Charbonneau lived.

1812 – Sacagawea died on December 12.

2000 – The United States released the commemorative Sacagawea Golden Dollar coin featuring Sacagawea and Pomp.

Sacagawea, Mother of Discovery

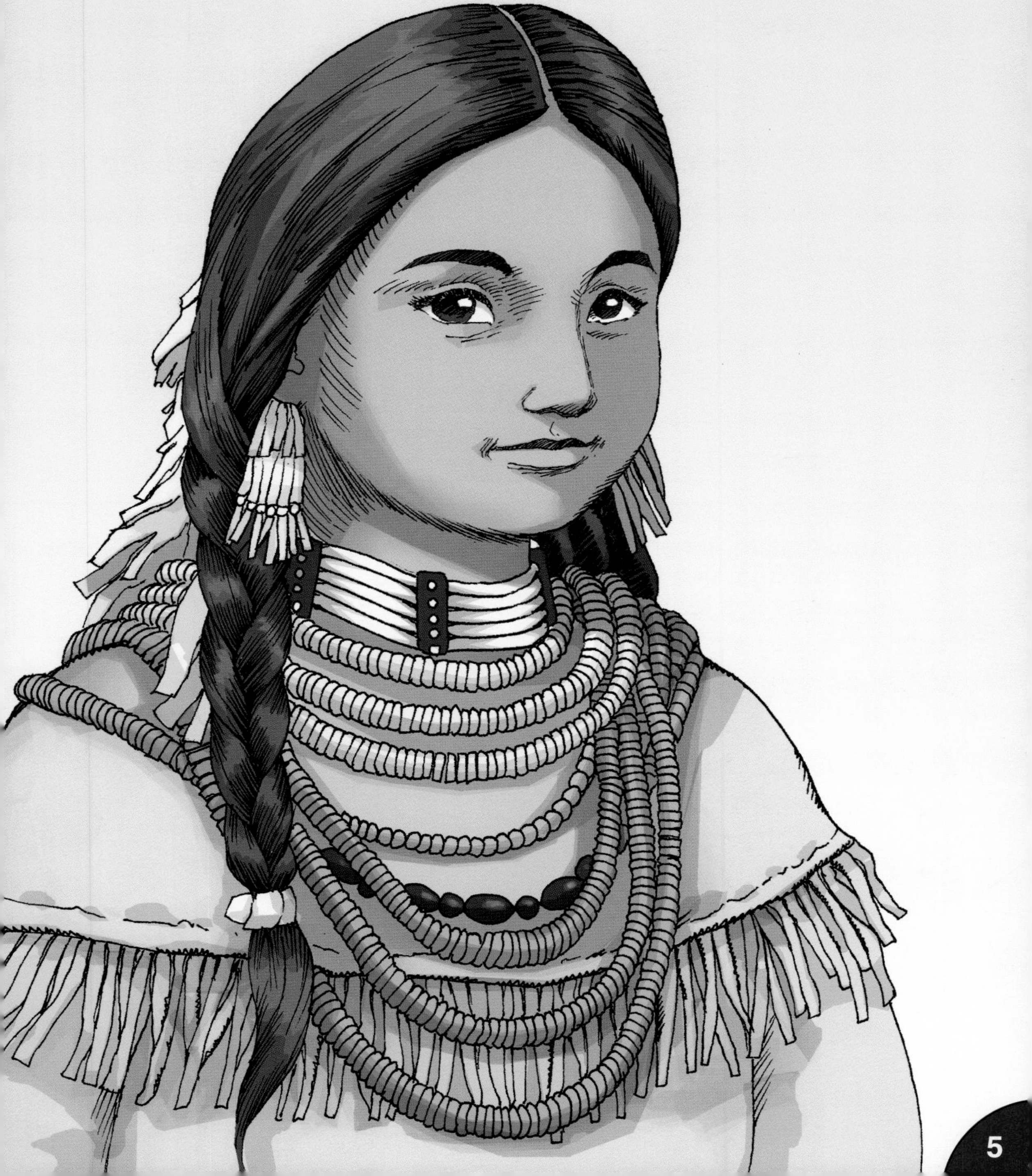

Chapter 1 Bird Woman

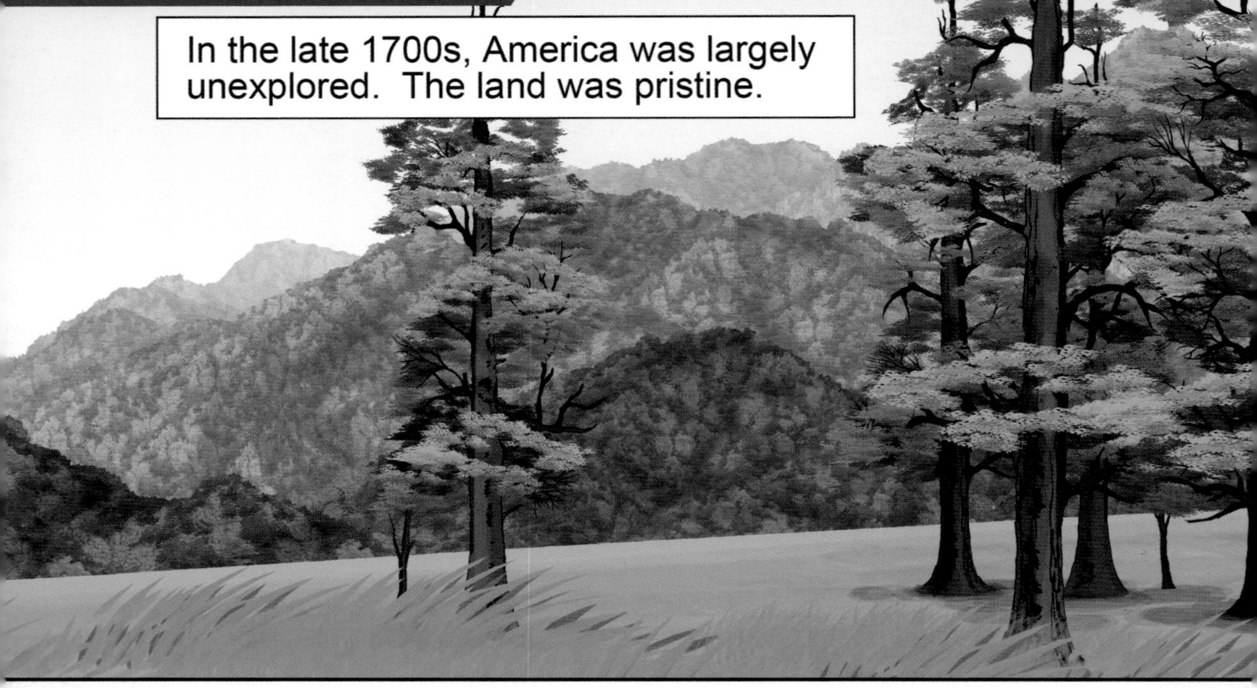

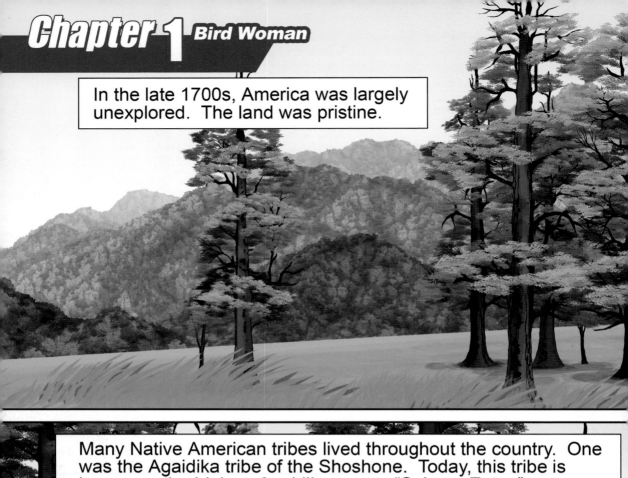

In the late 1700s, America was largely unexplored. The land was pristine.

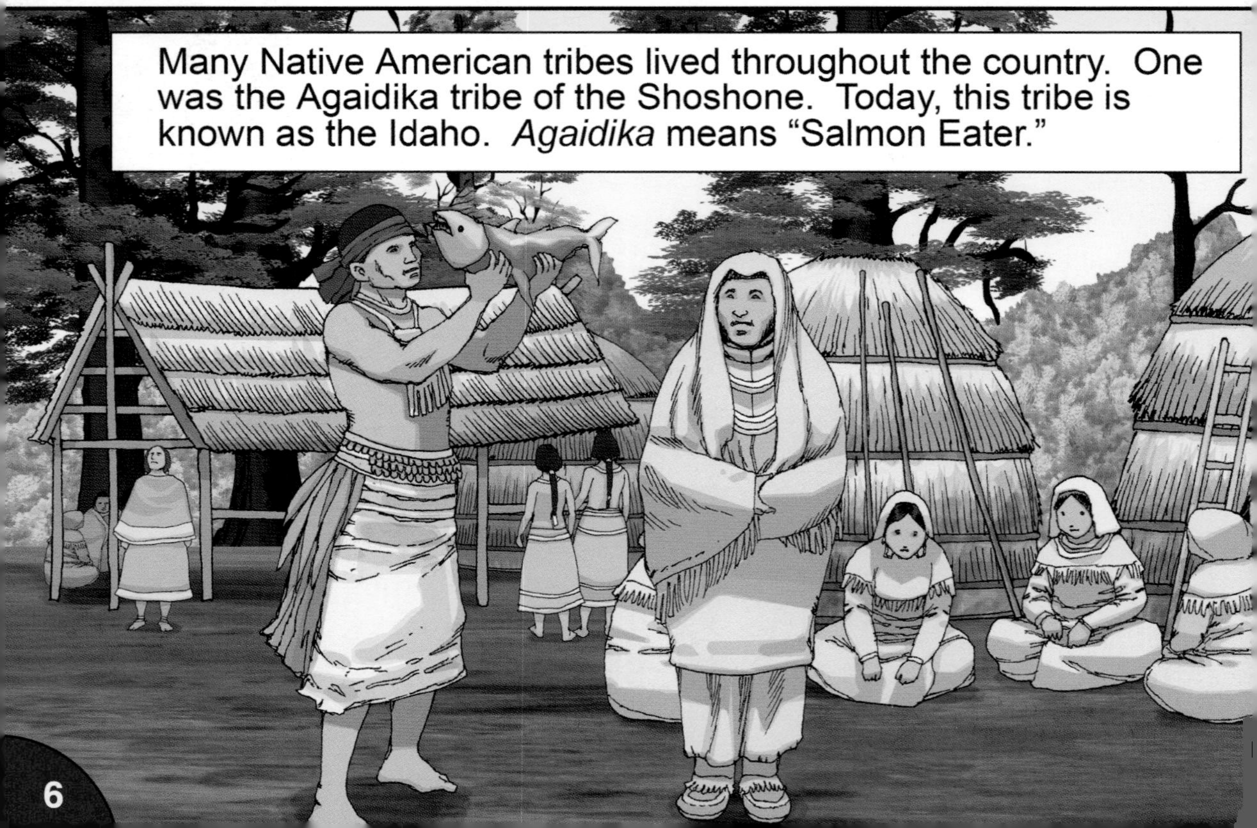

Many Native American tribes lived throughout the country. One was the Agaidika tribe of the Shoshone. Today, this tribe is known as the Idaho. *Agaidika* means "Salmon Eater."

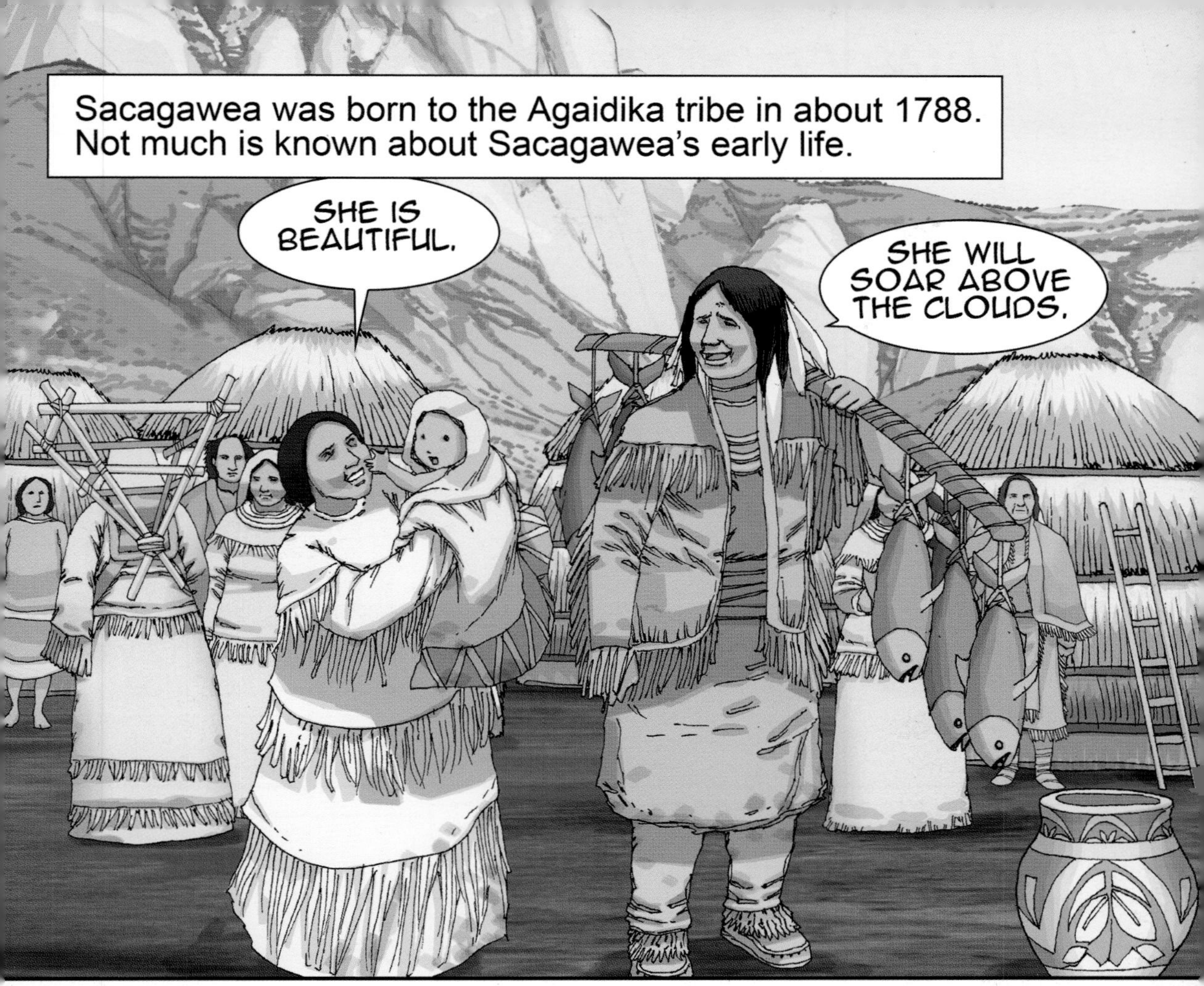

Sacagawea was born to the Agaidika tribe in about 1788. Not much is known about Sacagawea's early life.
SHE IS BEAUTIFUL.
SHE WILL SOAR ABOVE THE CLOUDS.

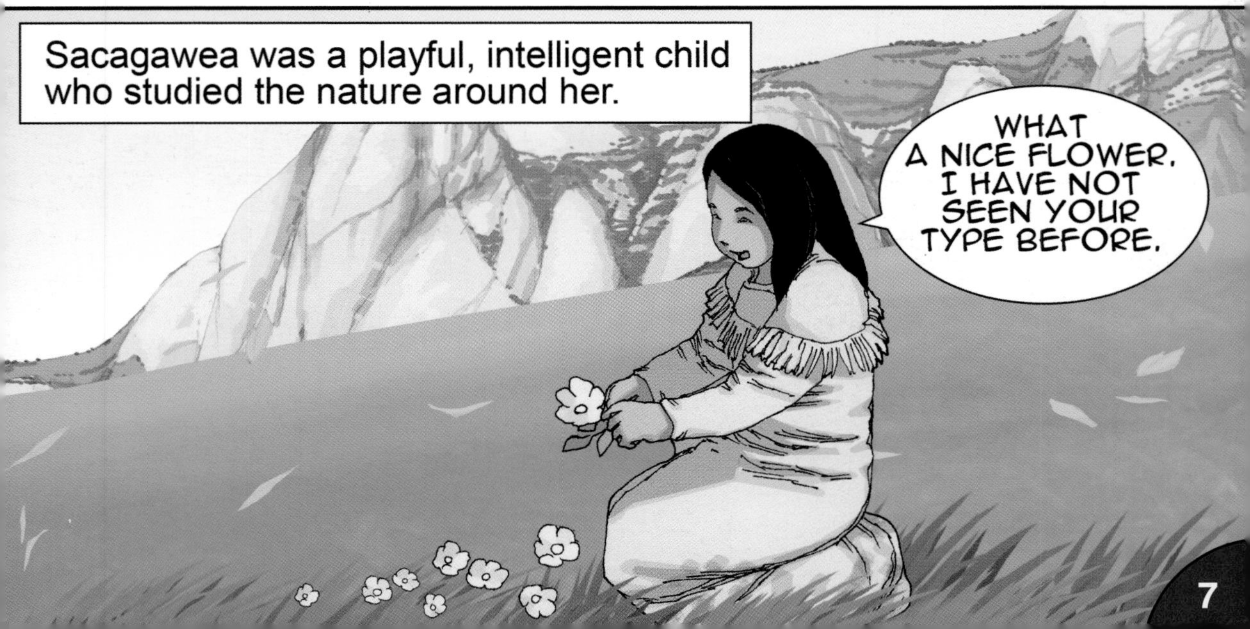

Sacagawea was a playful, intelligent child who studied the nature around her.
WHAT A NICE FLOWER. I HAVE NOT SEEN YOUR TYPE BEFORE.

Chapter 2 Married Life

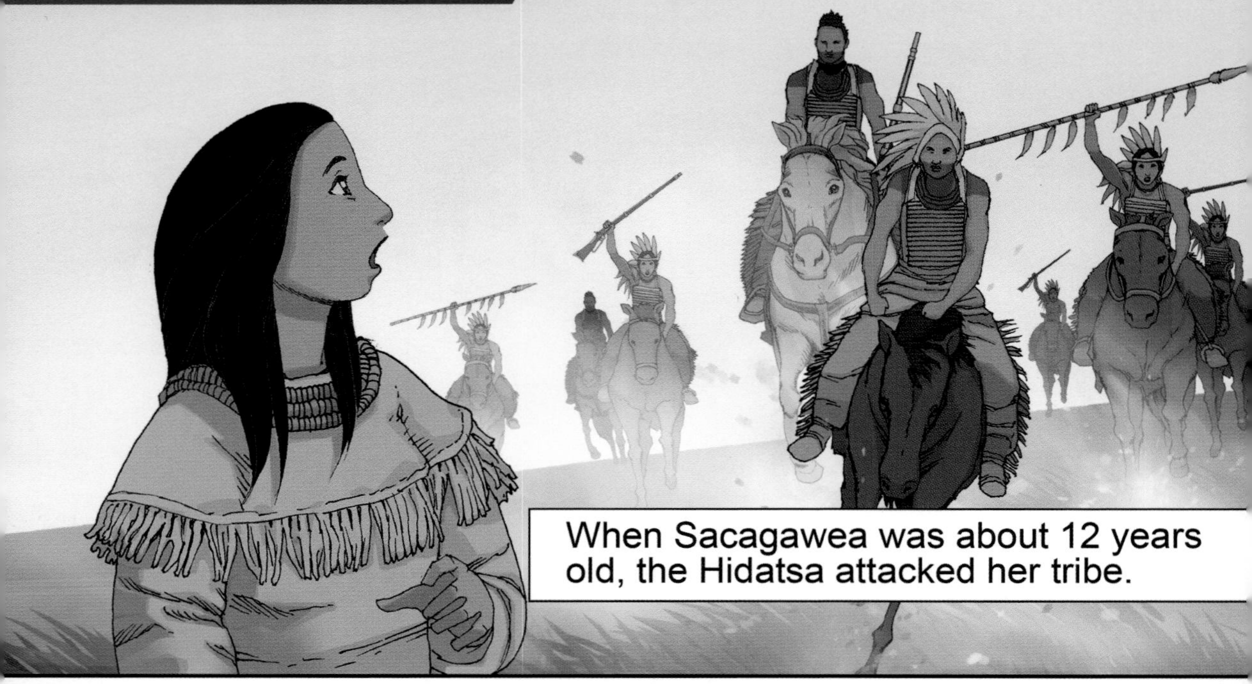
When Sacagawea was about 12 years old, the Hidatsa attacked her tribe.

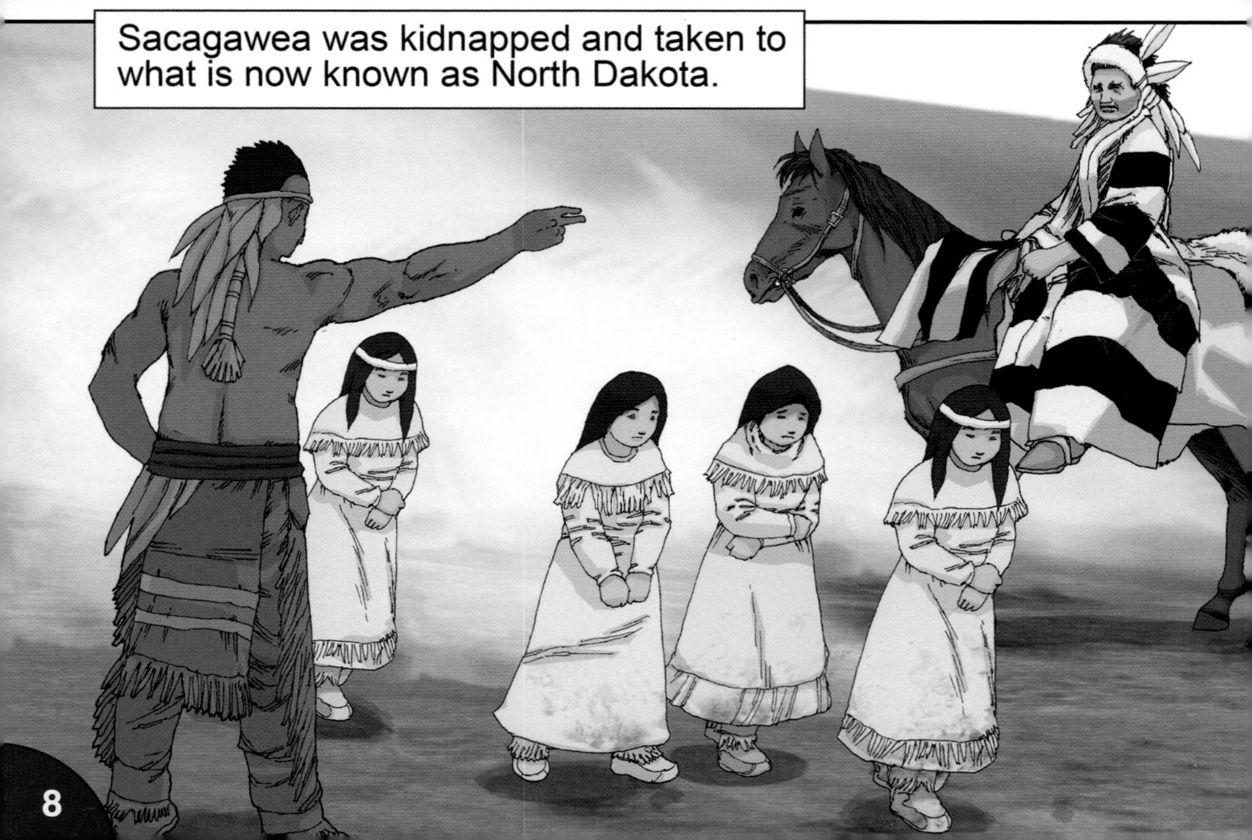
Sacagawea was kidnapped and taken to what is now known as North Dakota.

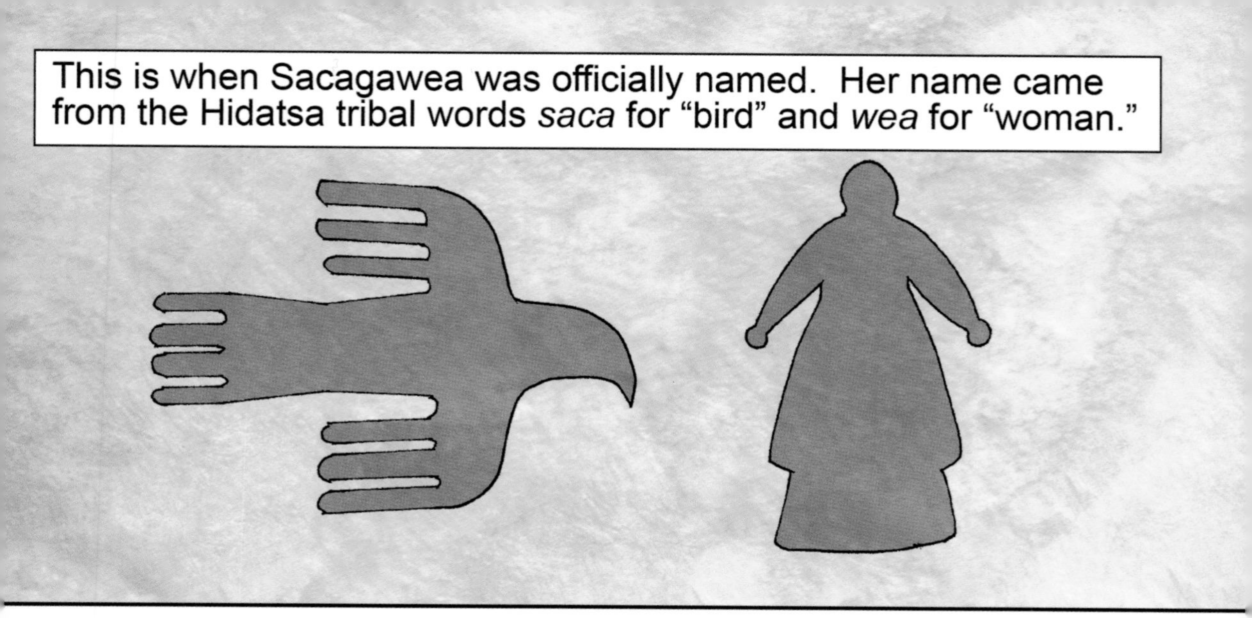
This is when Sacagawea was officially named. Her name came from the Hidatsa tribal words *saca* for "bird" and *wea* for "woman."

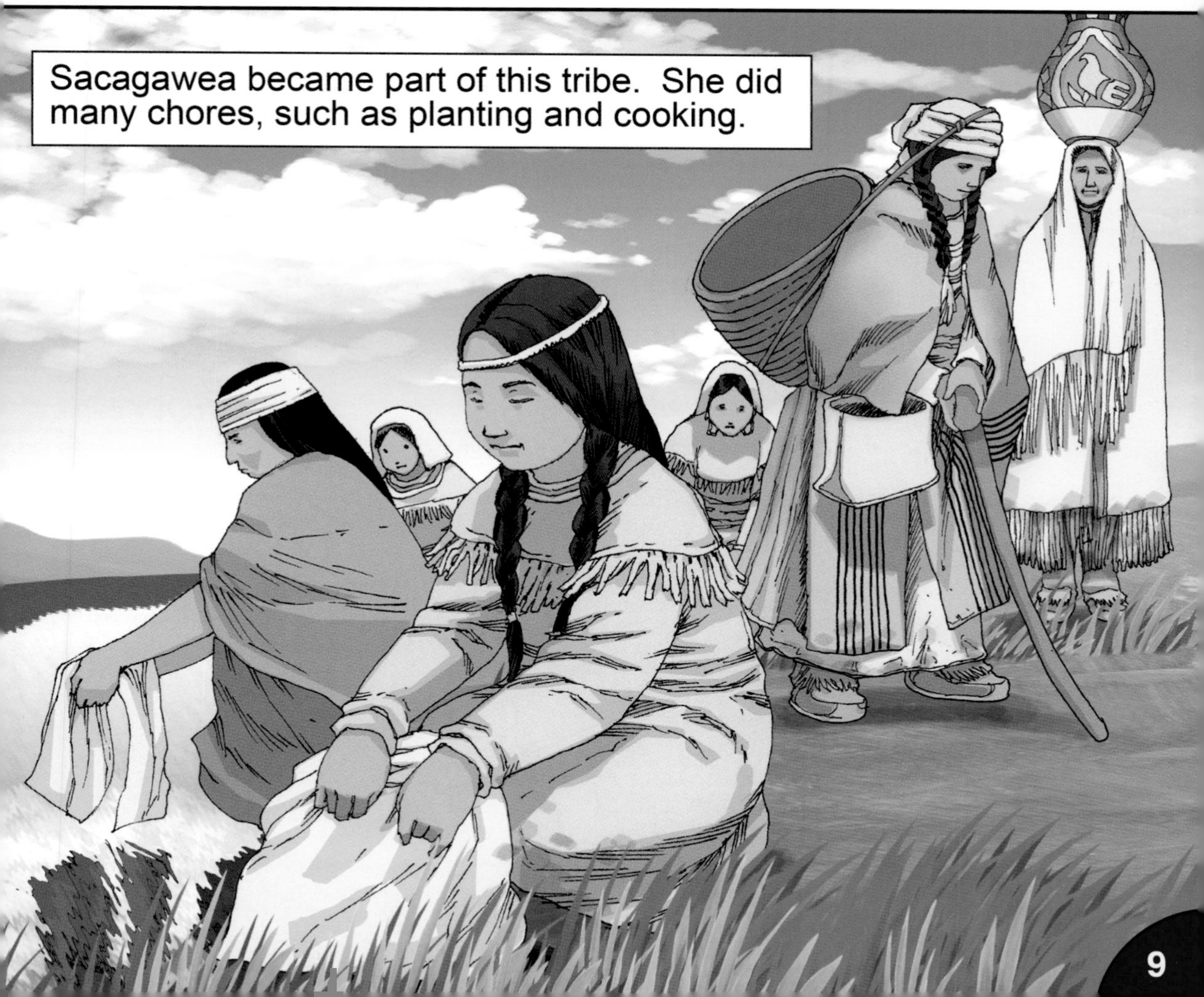
Sacagawea became part of this tribe. She did many chores, such as planting and cooking.

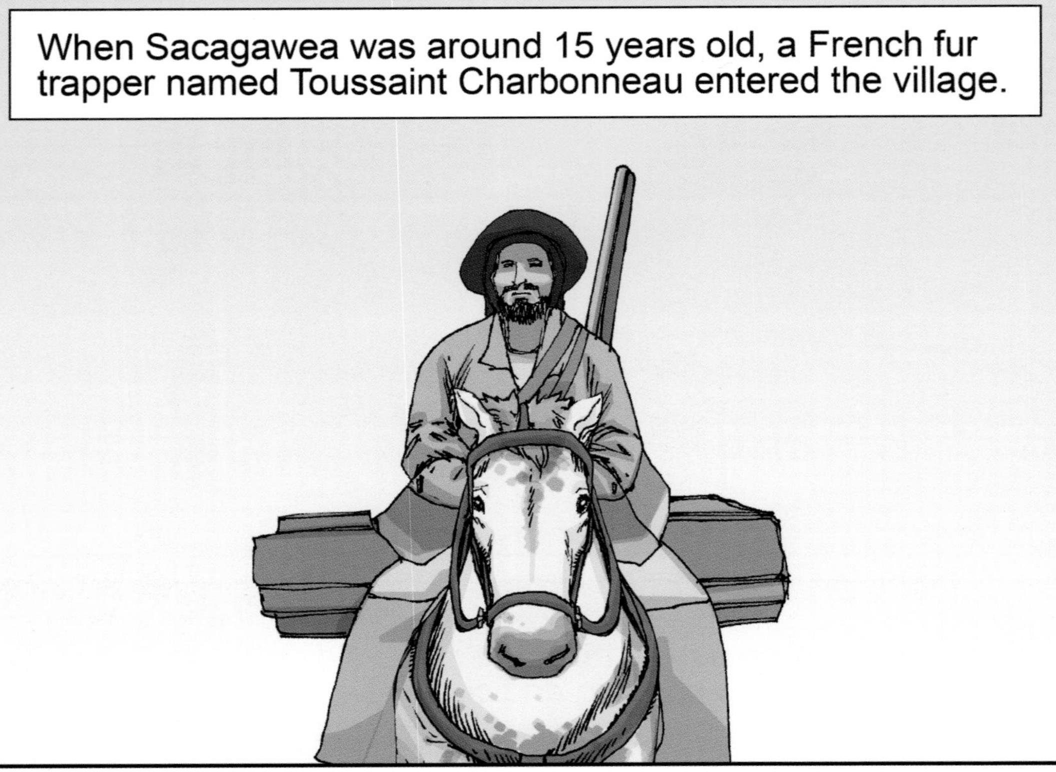
When Sacagawea was around 15 years old, a French fur trapper named Toussaint Charbonneau entered the village.

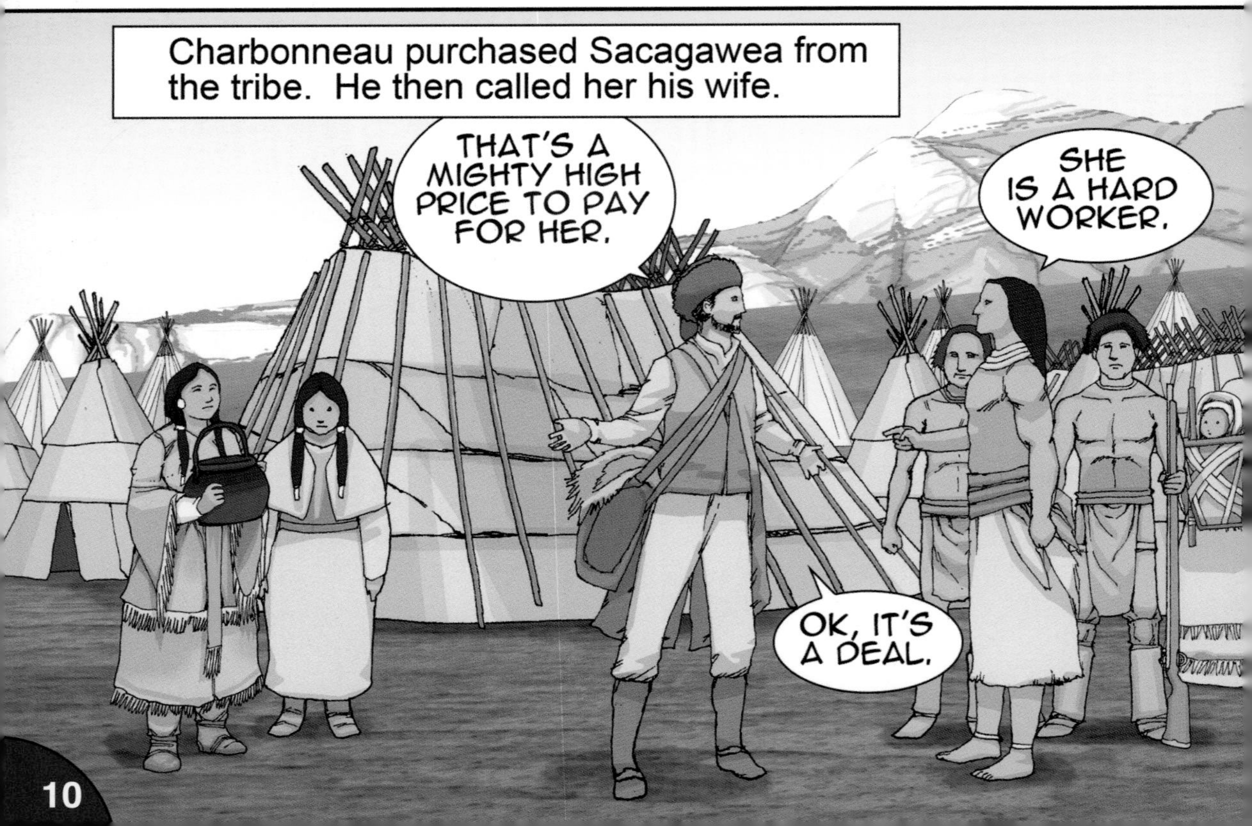
Charbonneau purchased Sacagawea from the tribe. He then called her his wife.
THAT'S A MIGHTY HIGH PRICE TO PAY FOR HER.
SHE IS A HARD WORKER.
OK, IT'S A DEAL.

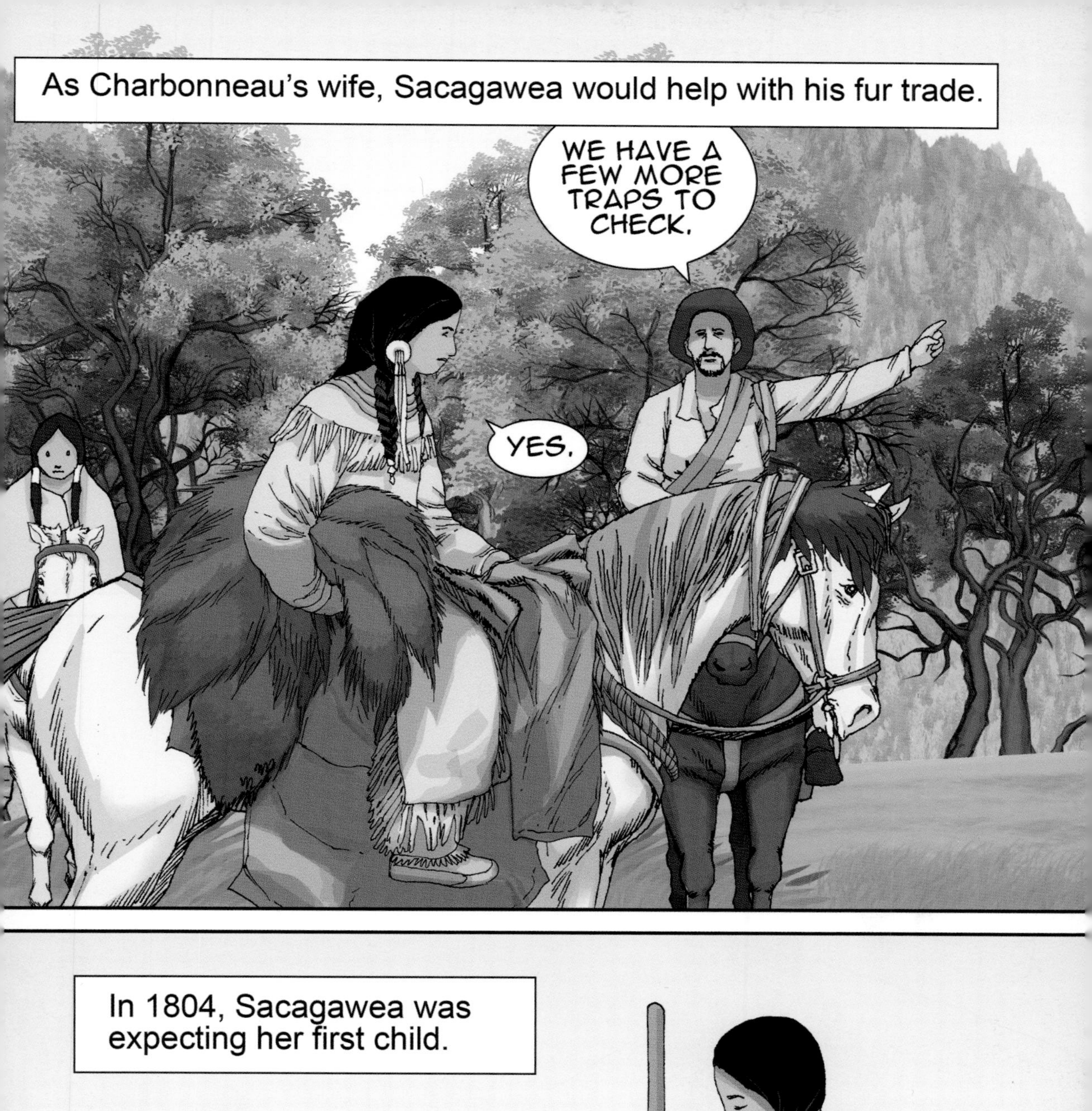
As Charbonneau's wife, Sacagawea would help with his fur trade.
WE HAVE A FEW MORE TRAPS TO CHECK.
YES.

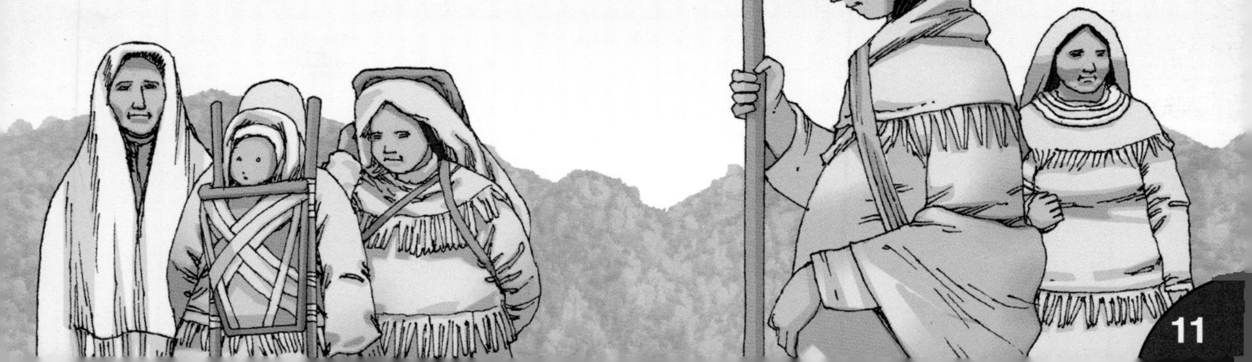
In 1804, Sacagawea was expecting her first child.

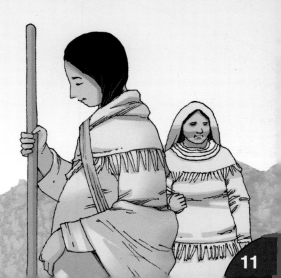

Chapter 3 The Corps of Discovery

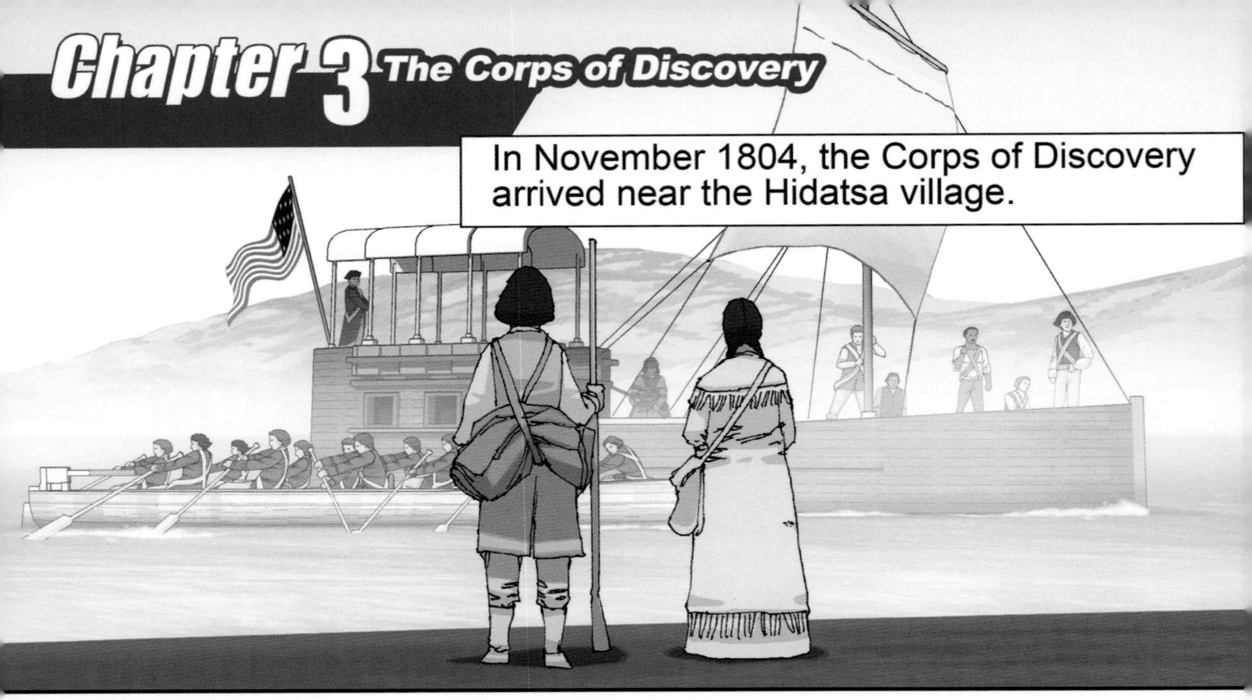
In November 1804, the Corps of Discovery arrived near the Hidatsa village.

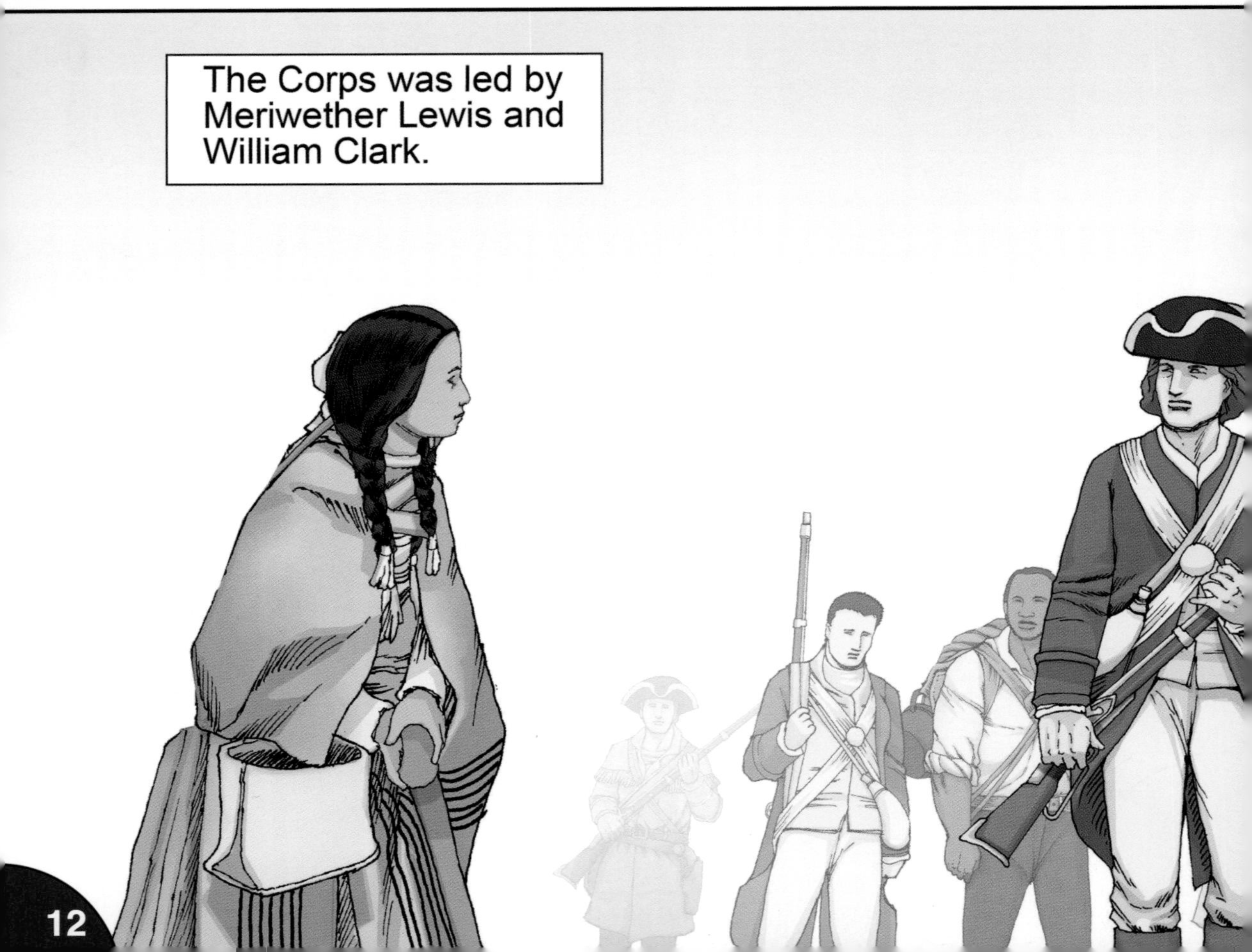
The Corps was led by Meriwether Lewis and William Clark.

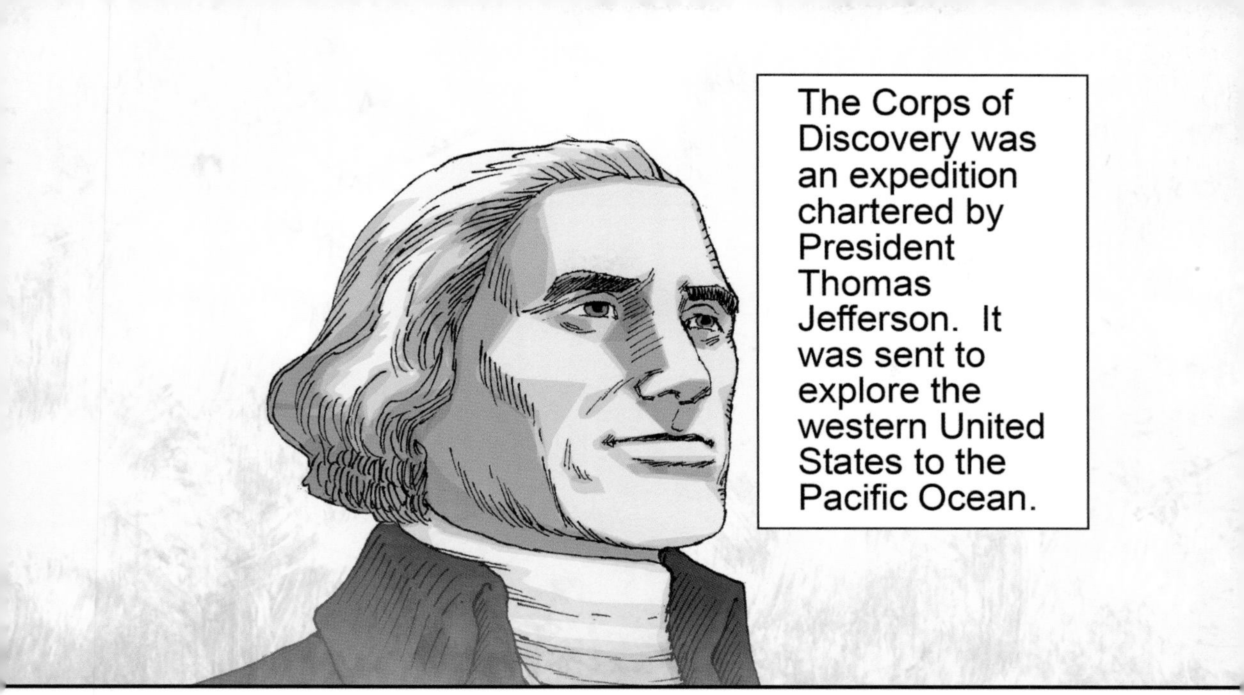
The Corps of Discovery was an expedition chartered by President Thomas Jefferson. It was sent to explore the western United States to the Pacific Ocean.

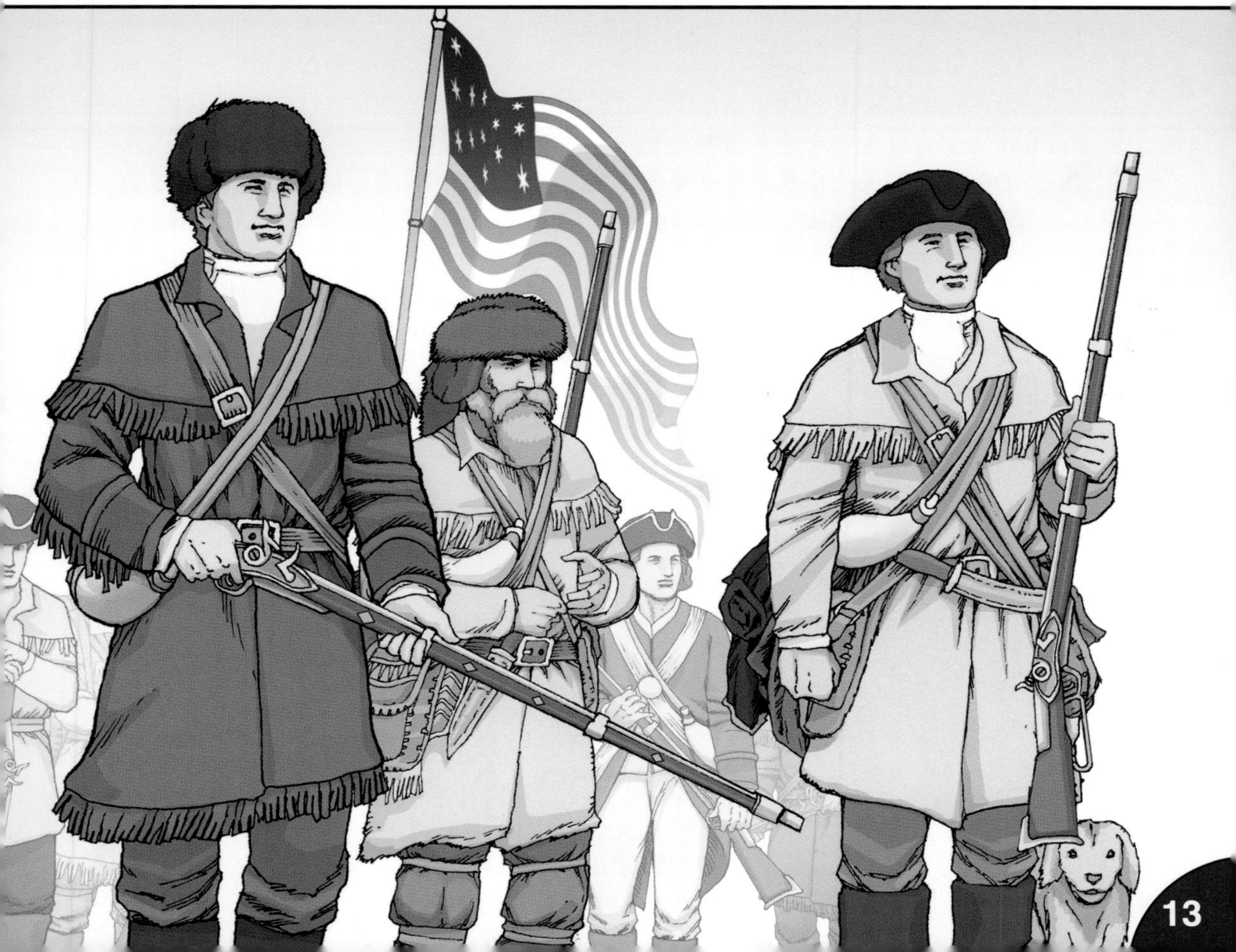

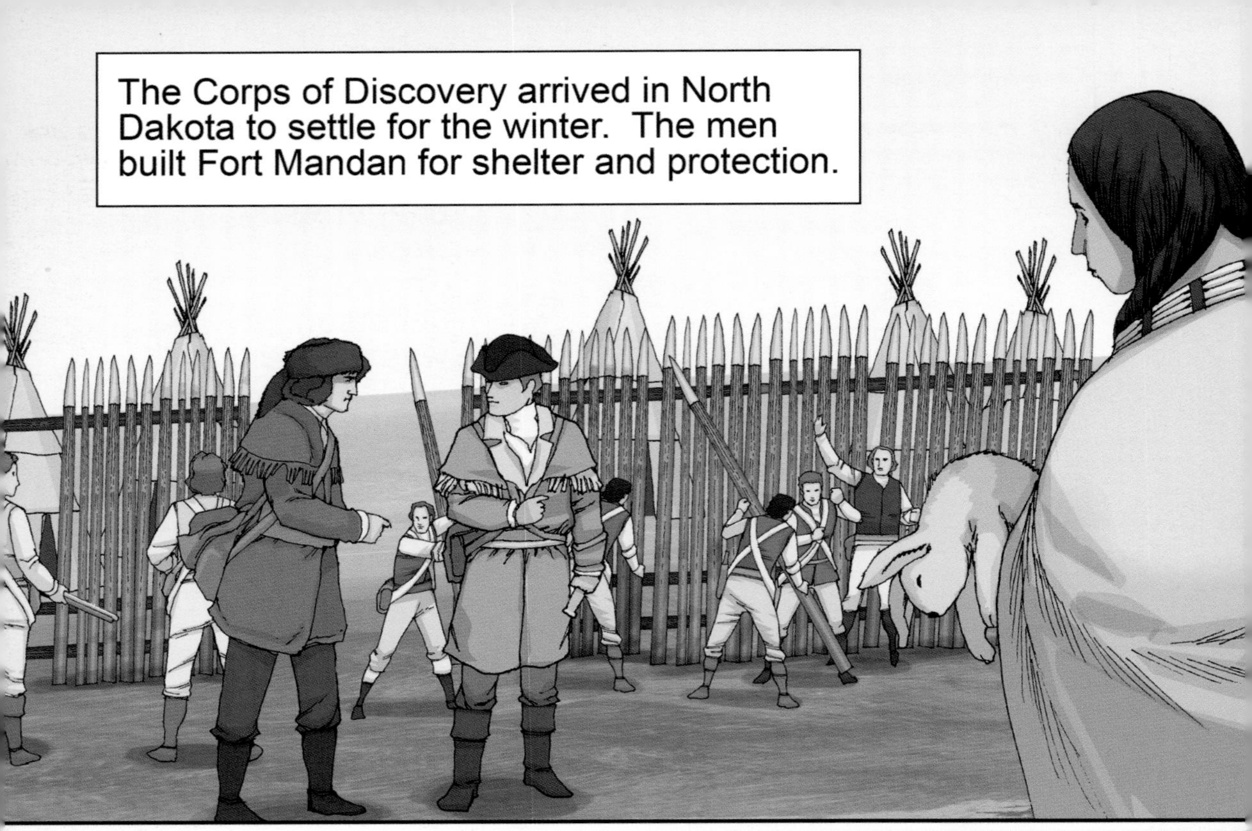
The Corps of Discovery arrived in North Dakota to settle for the winter. The men built Fort Mandan for shelter and protection.

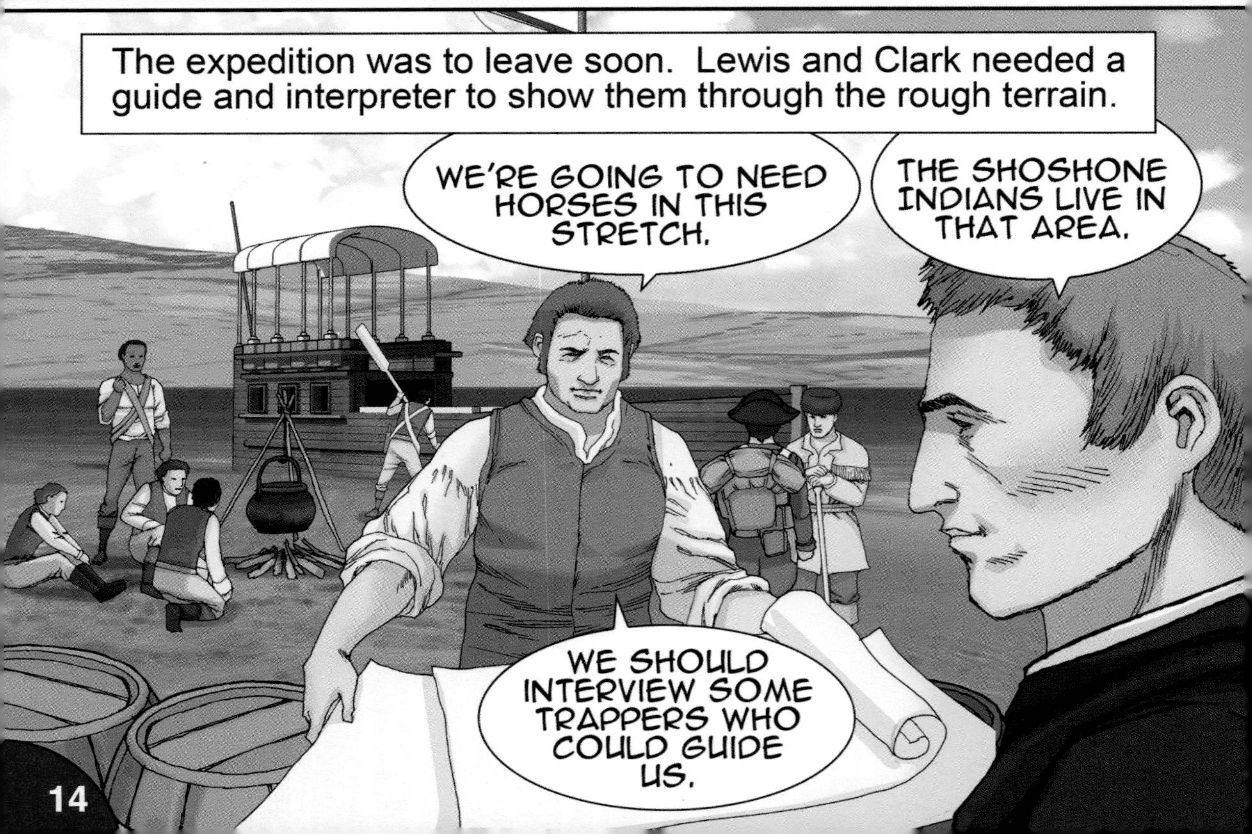
The expedition was to leave soon. Lewis and Clark needed a guide and interpreter to show them through the rough terrain.
WE'RE GOING TO NEED HORSES IN THIS STRETCH.
THE SHOSHONE INDIANS LIVE IN THAT AREA.
WE SHOULD INTERVIEW SOME TRAPPERS WHO COULD GUIDE US.

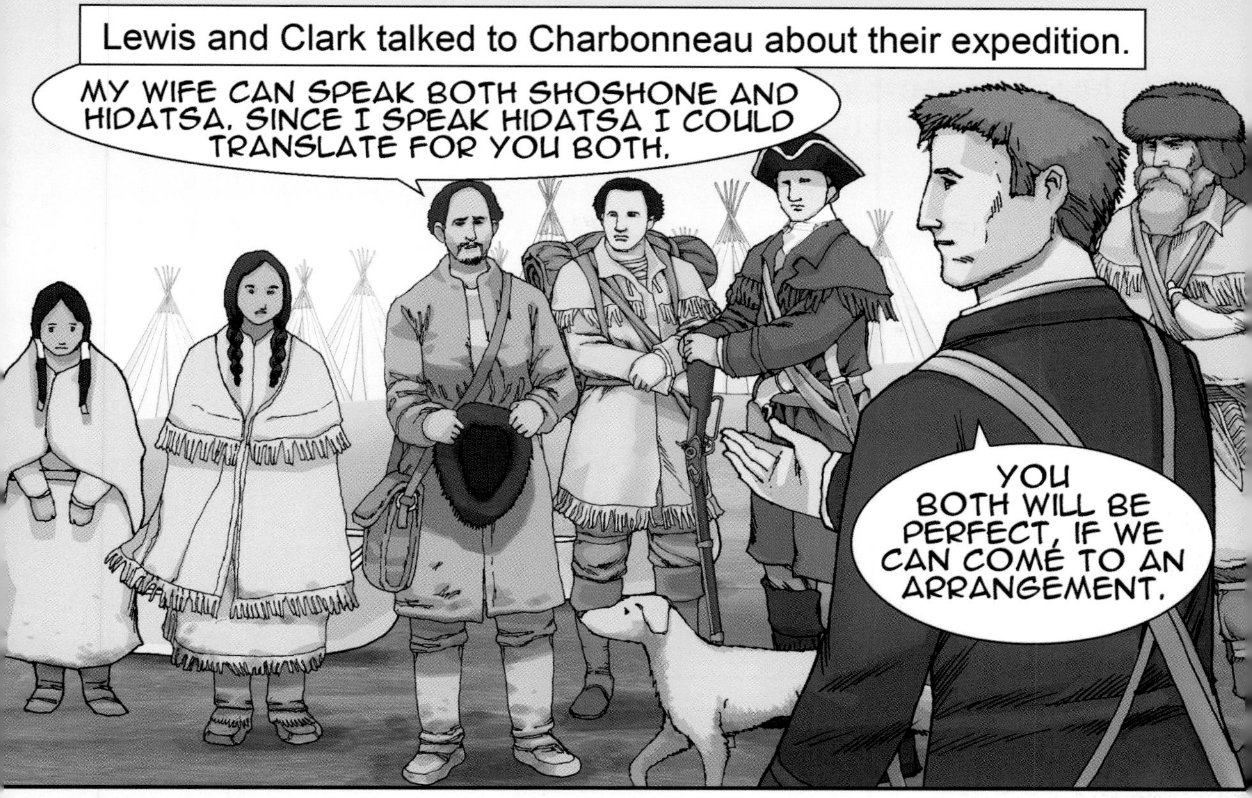
Lewis and Clark talked to Charbonneau about their expedition.
MY WIFE CAN SPEAK BOTH SHOSHONE AND HIDATSA. SINCE I SPEAK HIDATSA I COULD TRANSLATE FOR YOU BOTH.
YOU BOTH WILL BE PERFECT, IF WE CAN COME TO AN ARRANGEMENT.

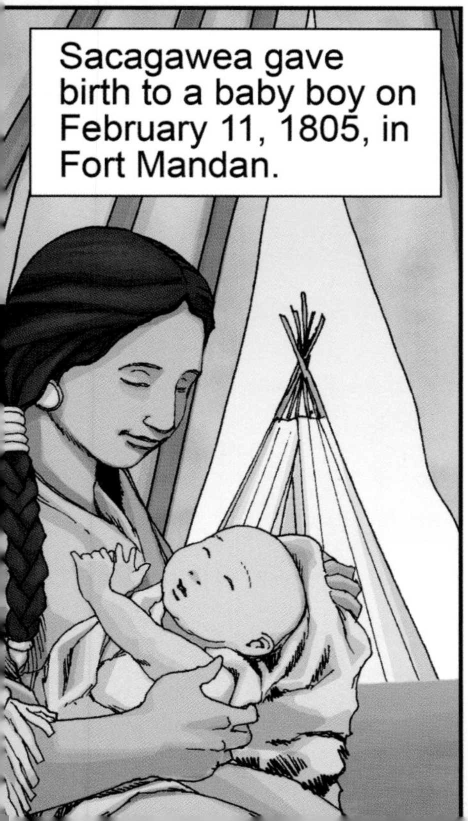
Sacagawea gave birth to a baby boy on February 11, 1805, in Fort Mandan.

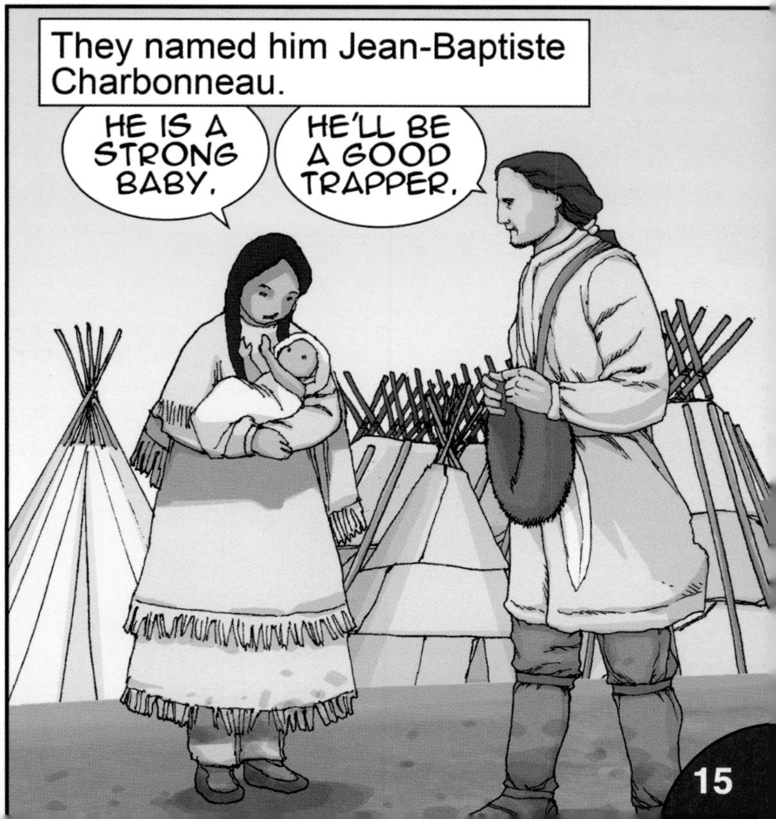
They named him Jean-Baptiste Charbonneau.
HE IS A STRONG BABY.
HE'LL BE A GOOD TRAPPER.

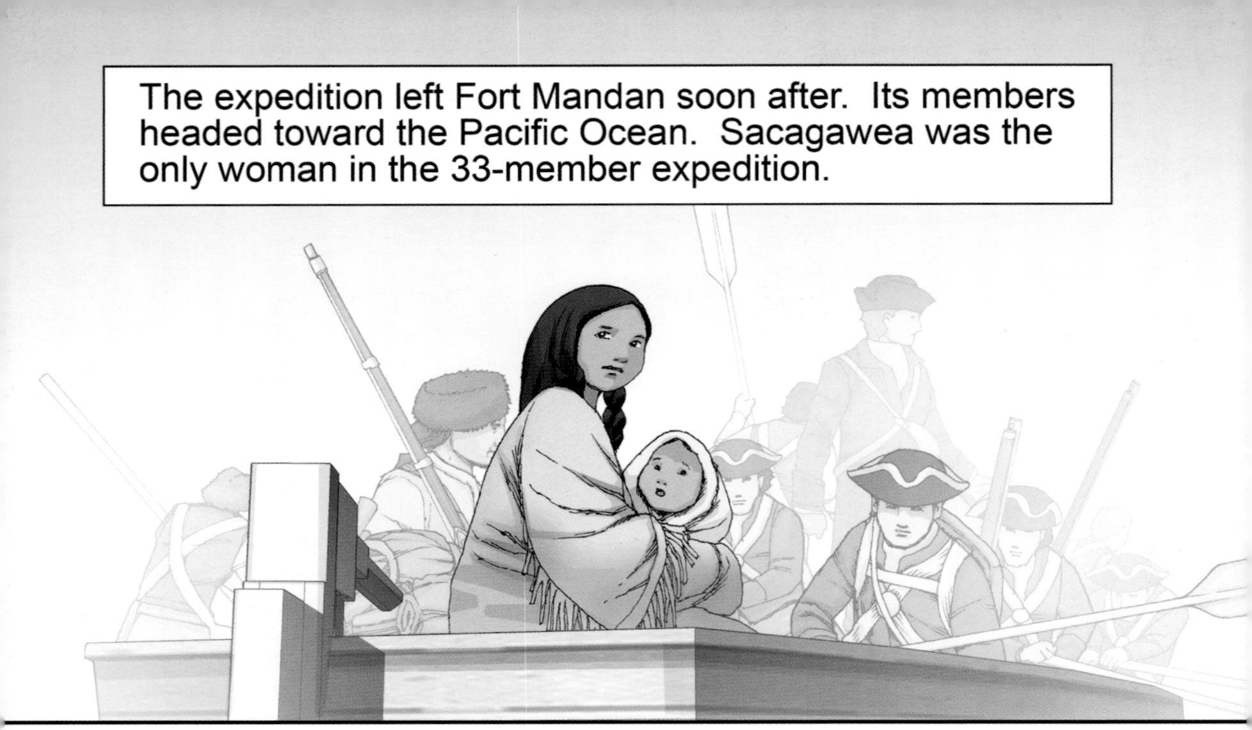
The expedition left Fort Mandan soon after. Its members headed toward the Pacific Ocean. Sacagawea was the only woman in the 33-member expedition.

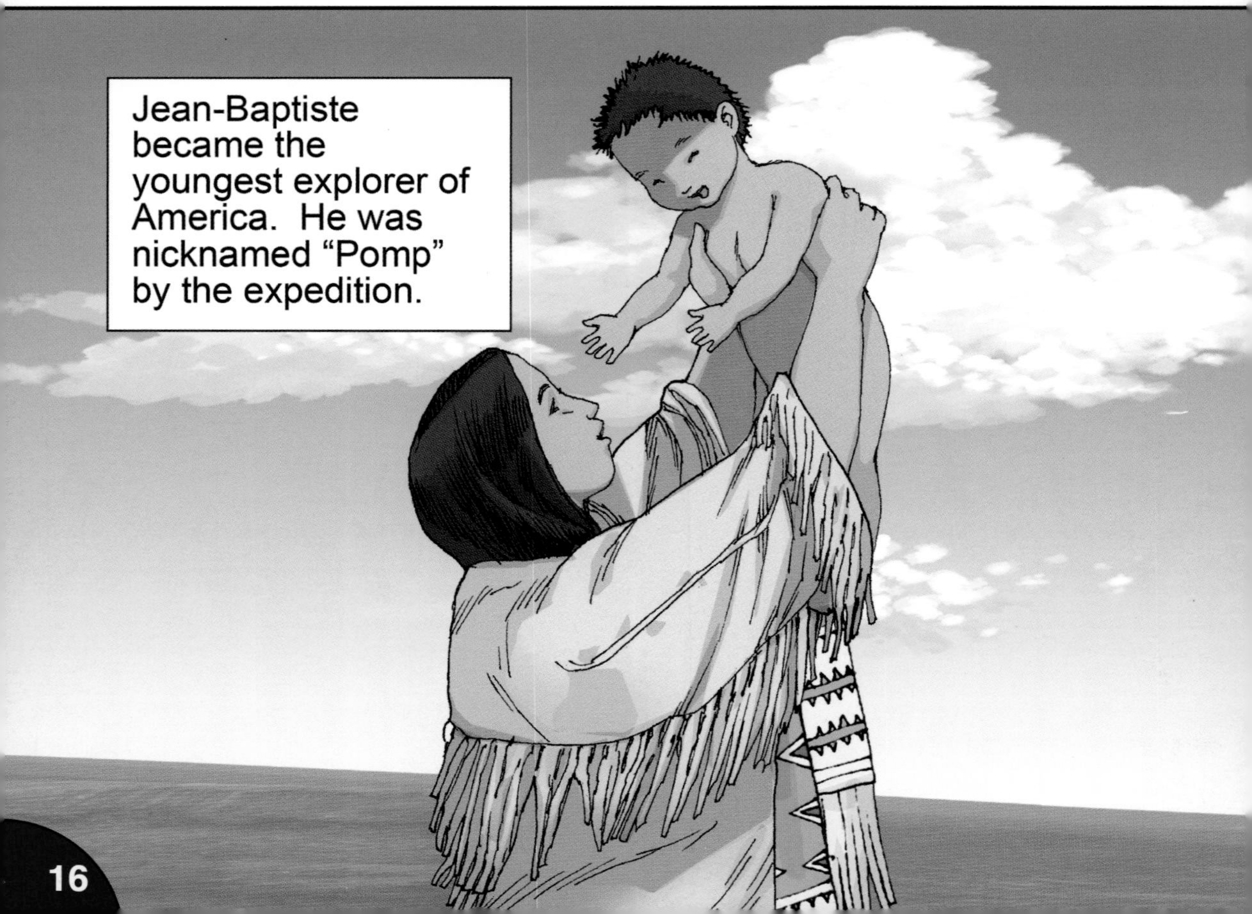
Jean-Baptiste became the youngest explorer of America. He was nicknamed "Pomp" by the expedition.

Chapter 4 Homecoming

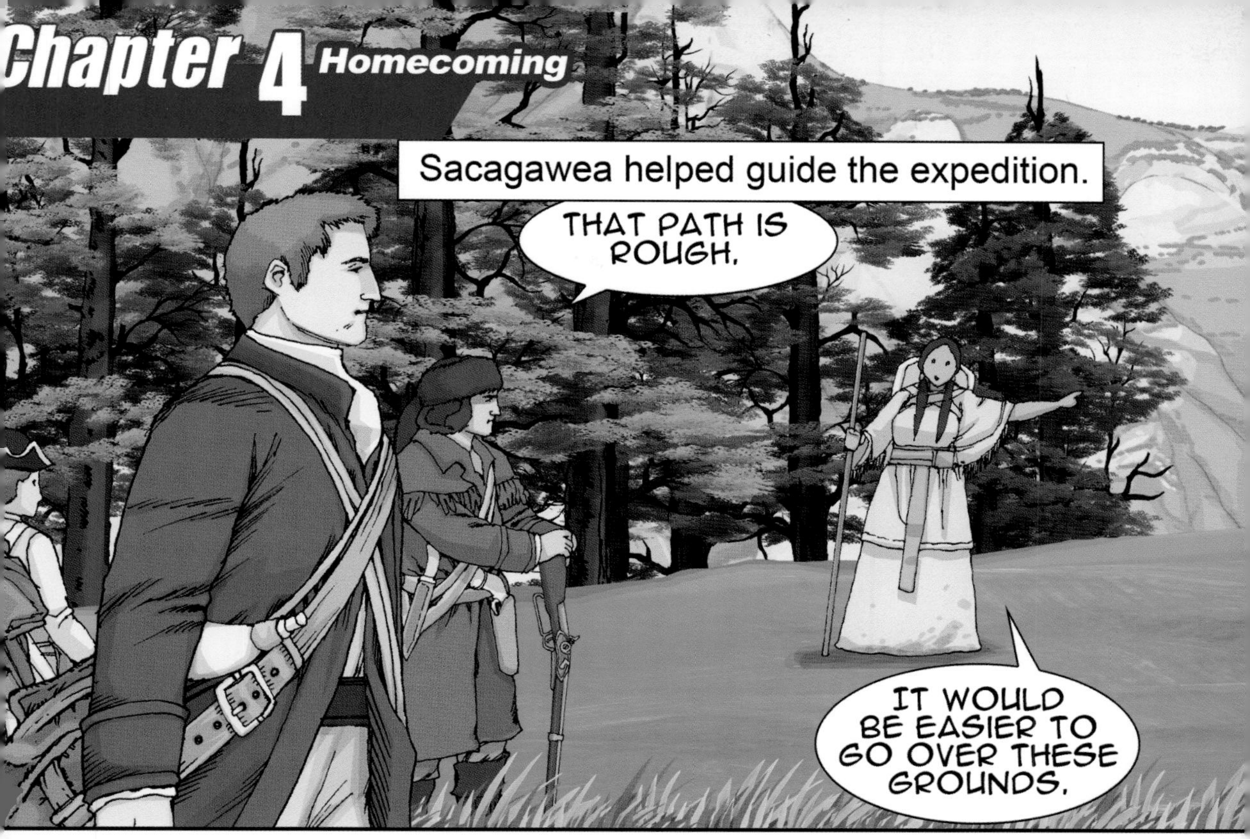
Sacagawea helped guide the expedition.
THAT PATH IS ROUGH.
IT WOULD BE EASIER TO GO OVER THESE GROUNDS.

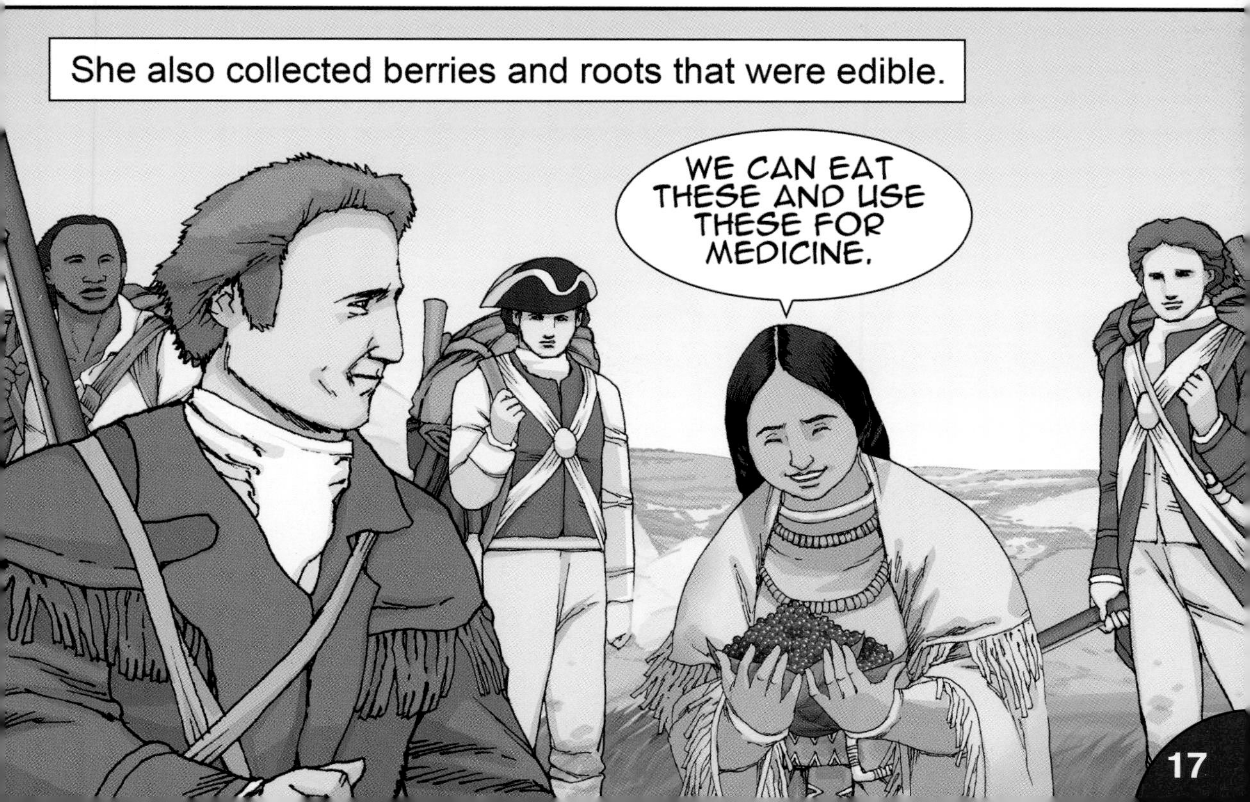
She also collected berries and roots that were edible.
WE CAN EAT THESE AND USE THESE FOR MEDICINE.

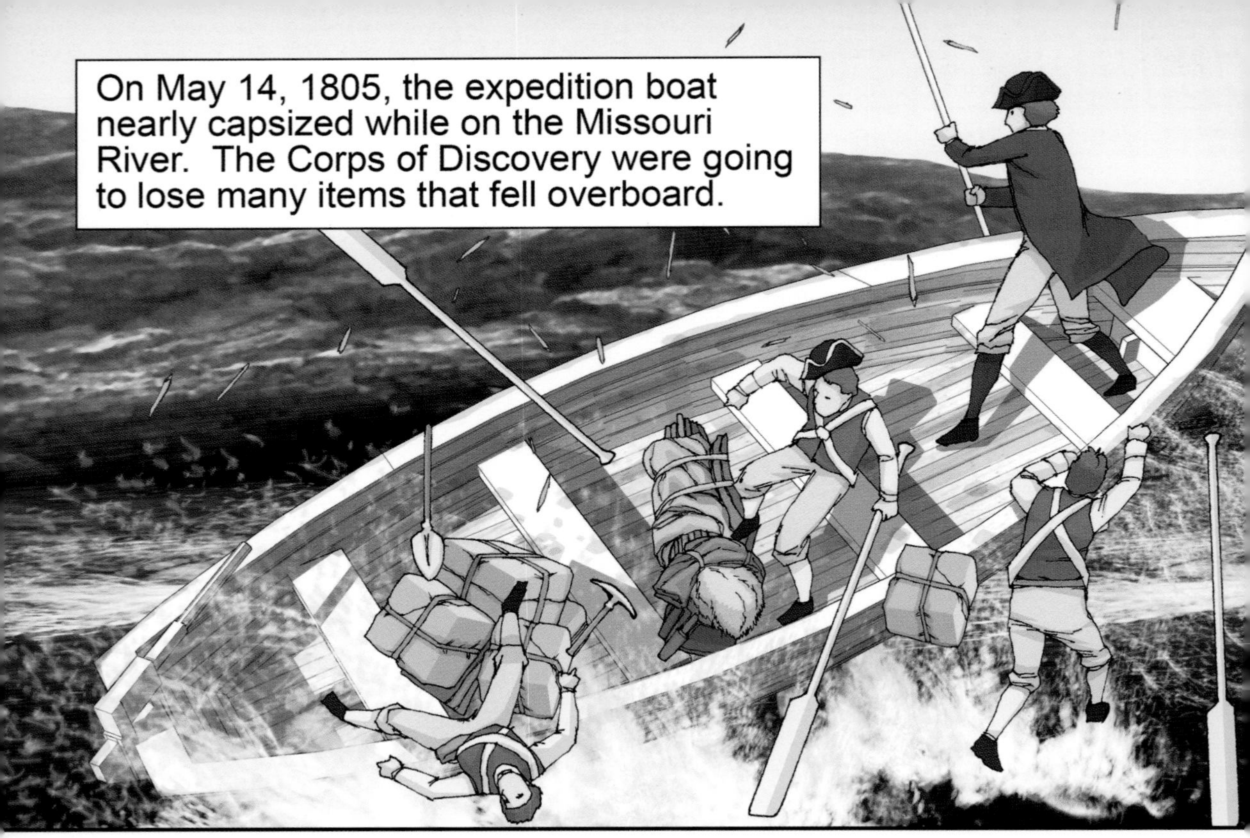
On May 14, 1805, the expedition boat nearly capsized while on the Missouri River. The Corps of Discovery were going to lose many items that fell overboard.

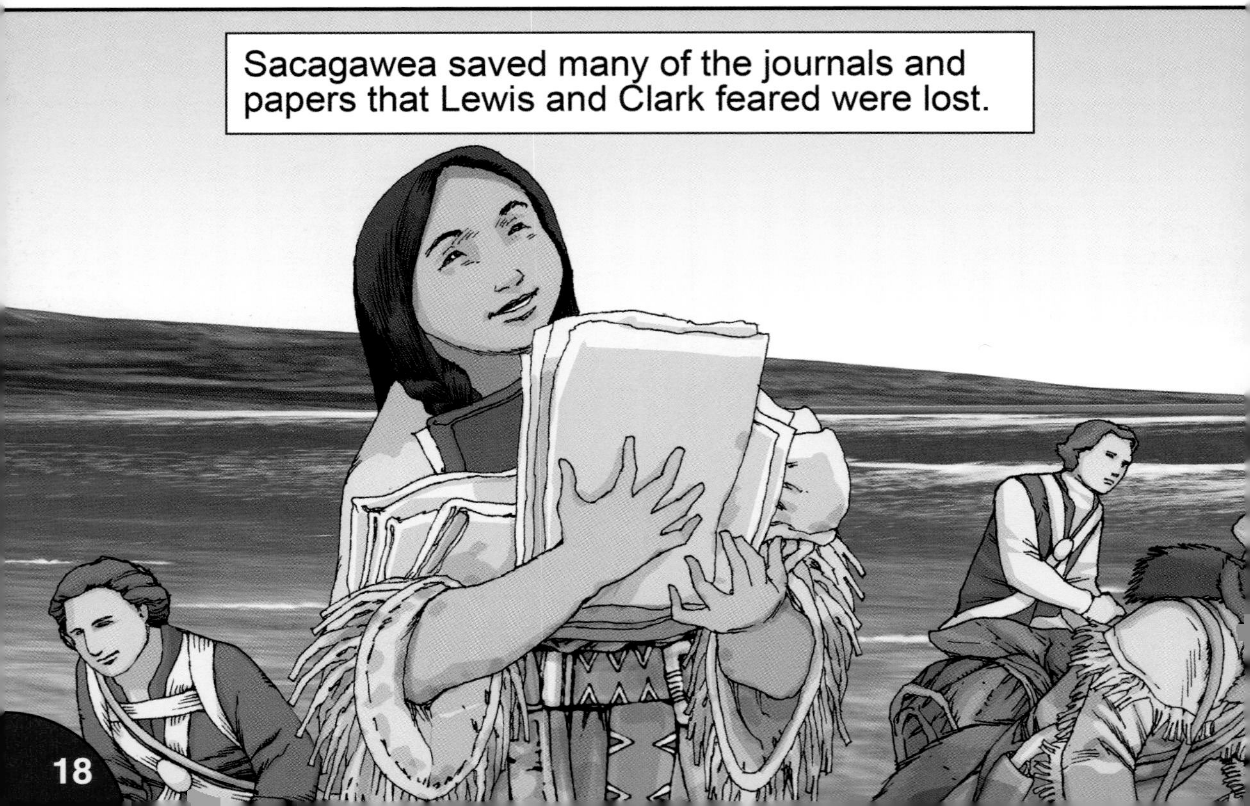
Sacagawea saved many of the journals and papers that Lewis and Clark feared were lost.

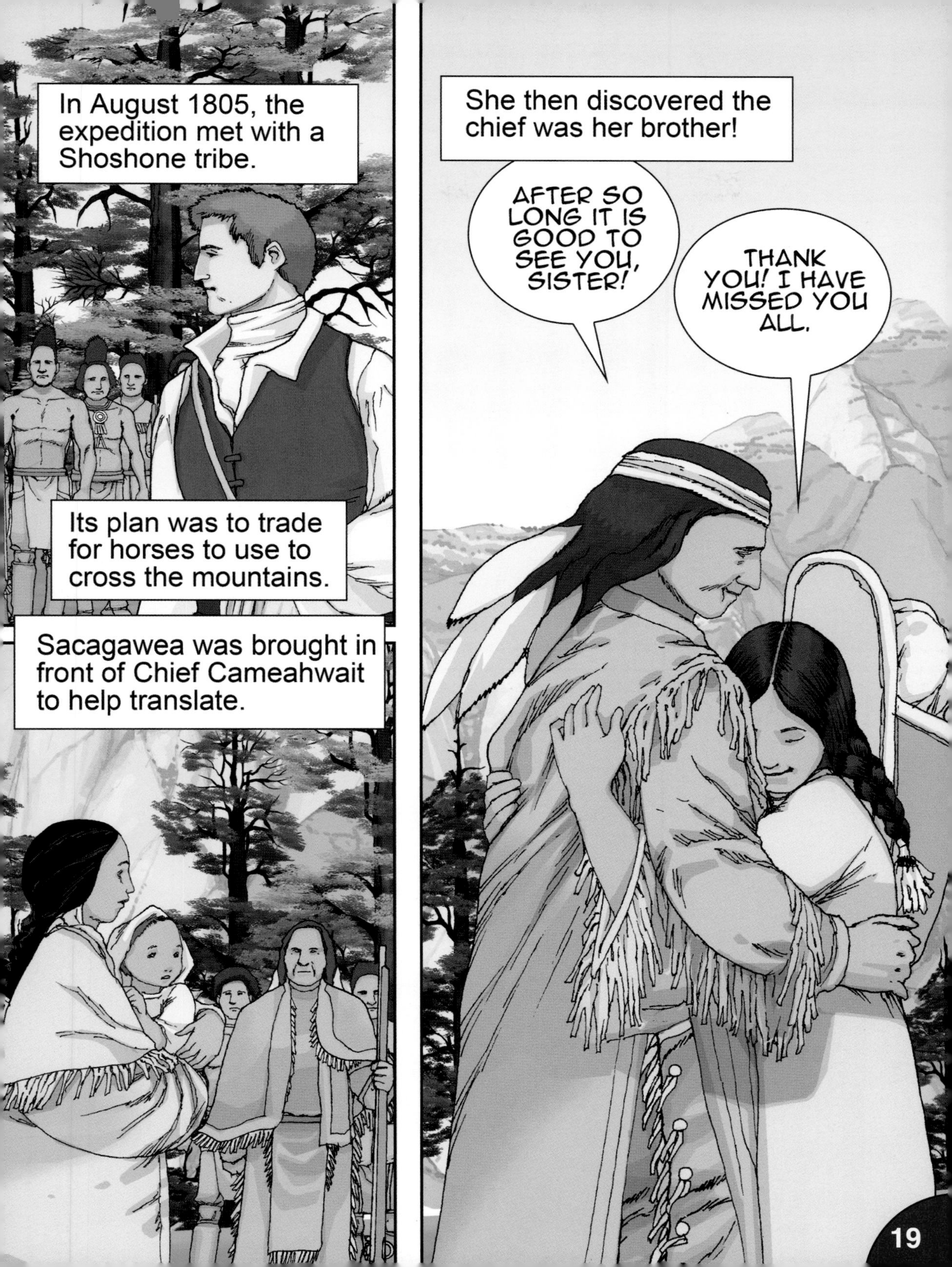
In August 1805, the expedition met with a Shoshone tribe.
Its plan was to trade for horses to use to cross the mountains.
Sacagawea was brought in front of Chief Cameahwait to help translate.
She then discovered the chief was her brother!
AFTER SO LONG IT IS GOOD TO SEE YOU, SISTER!
THANK YOU! I HAVE MISSED YOU ALL.

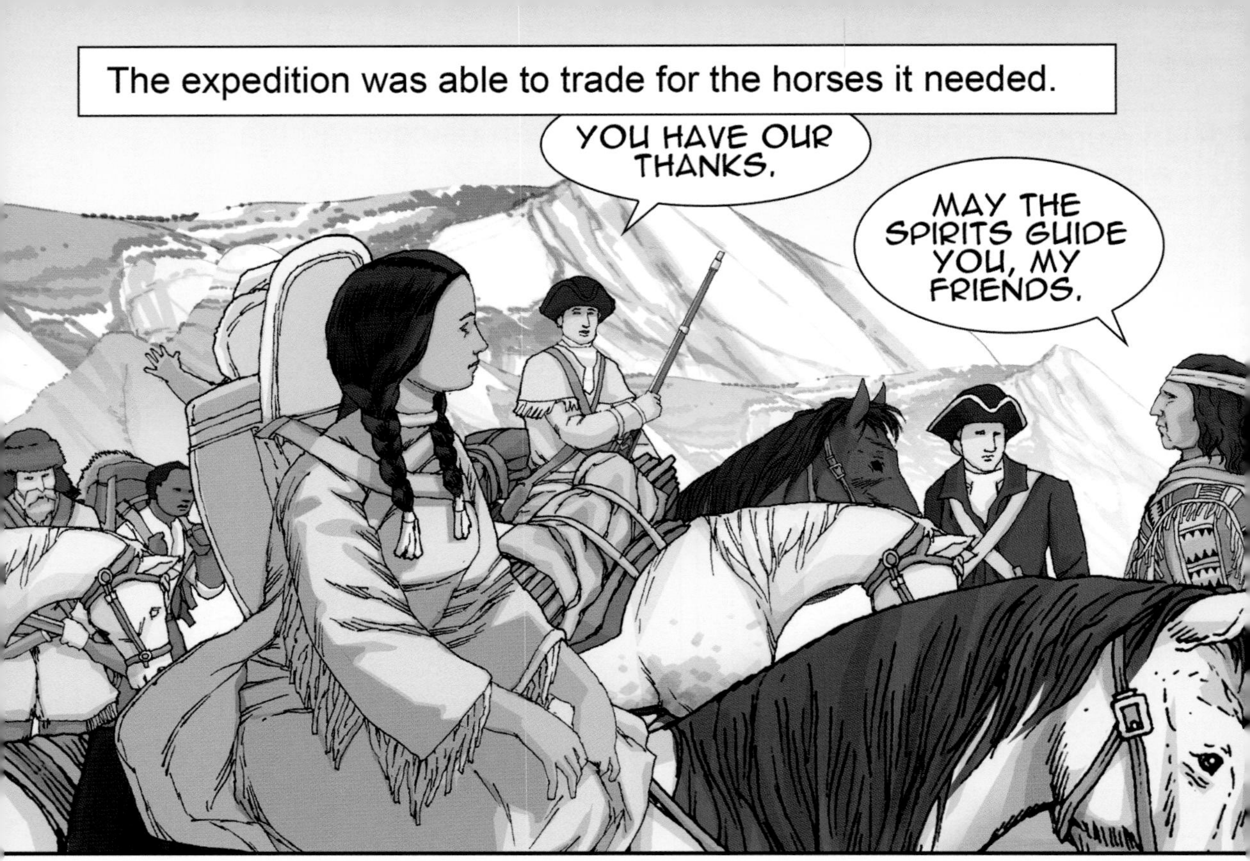
The expedition was able to trade for the horses it needed.
YOU HAVE OUR THANKS.
MAY THE SPIRITS GUIDE YOU, MY FRIENDS.

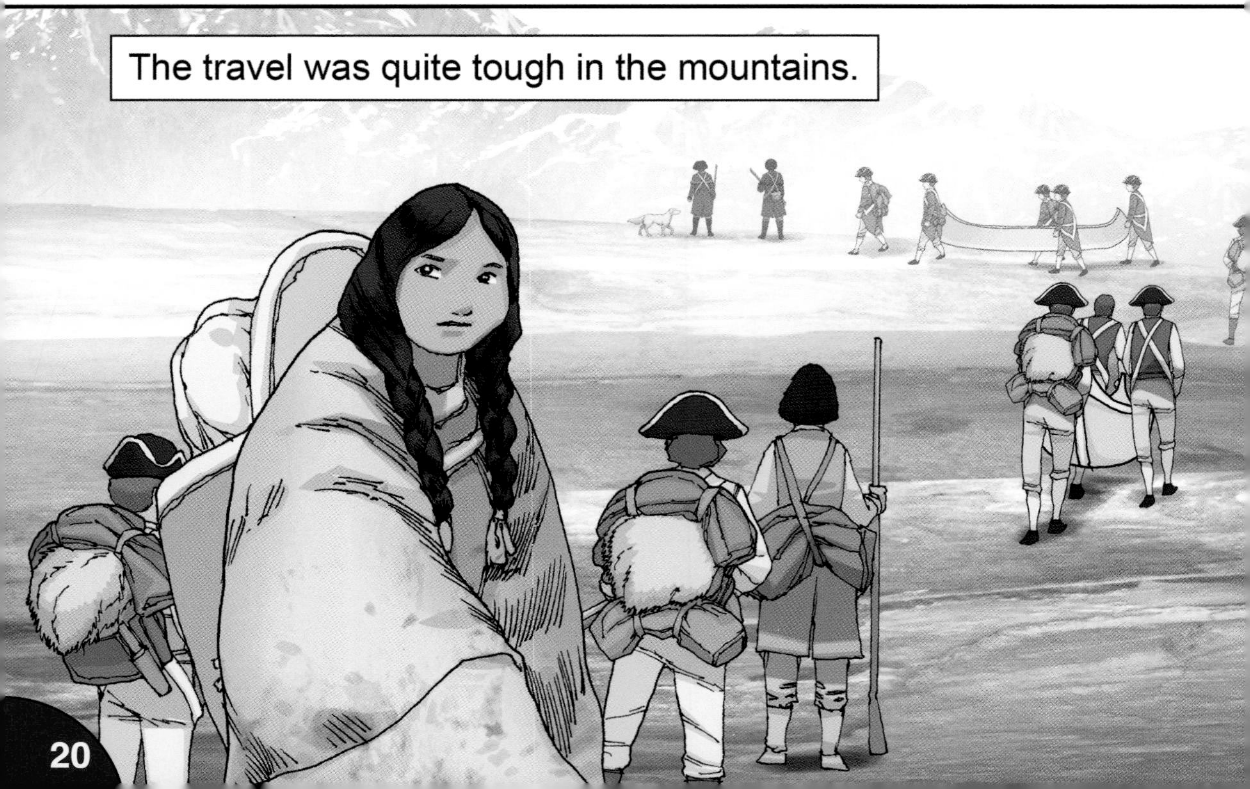
The travel was quite tough in the mountains.

Chapter 5 Enduring Many Hardships

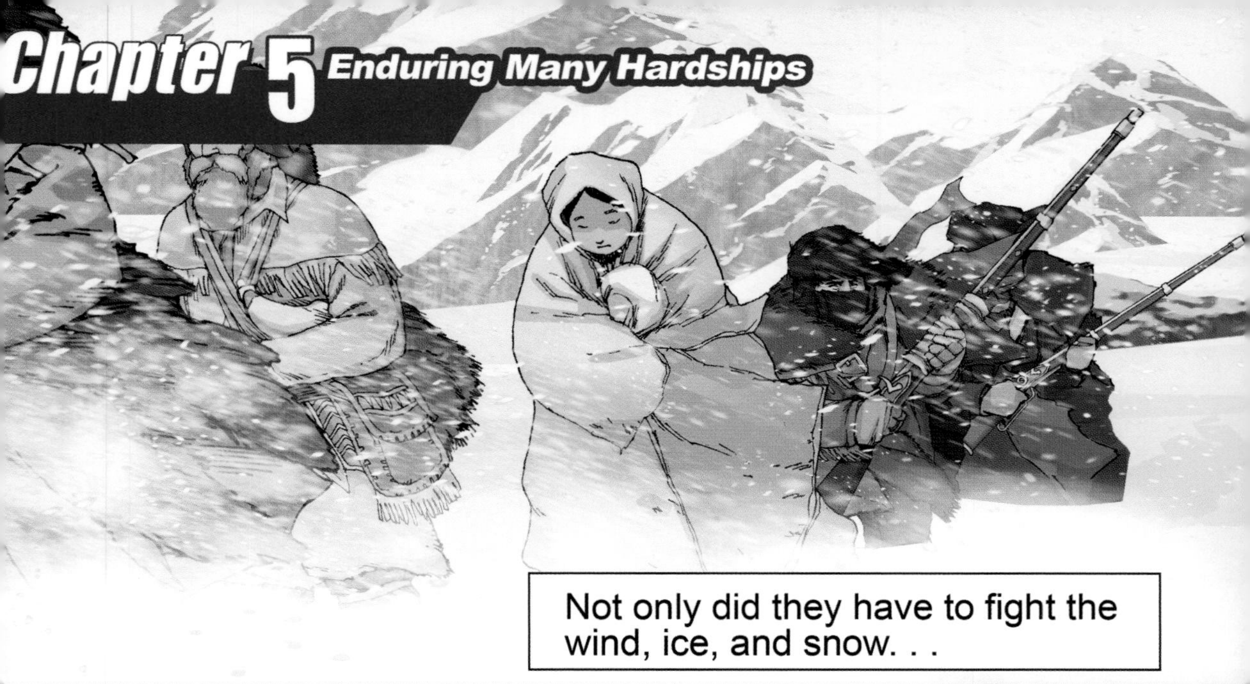
Not only did they have to fight the wind, ice, and snow. . .

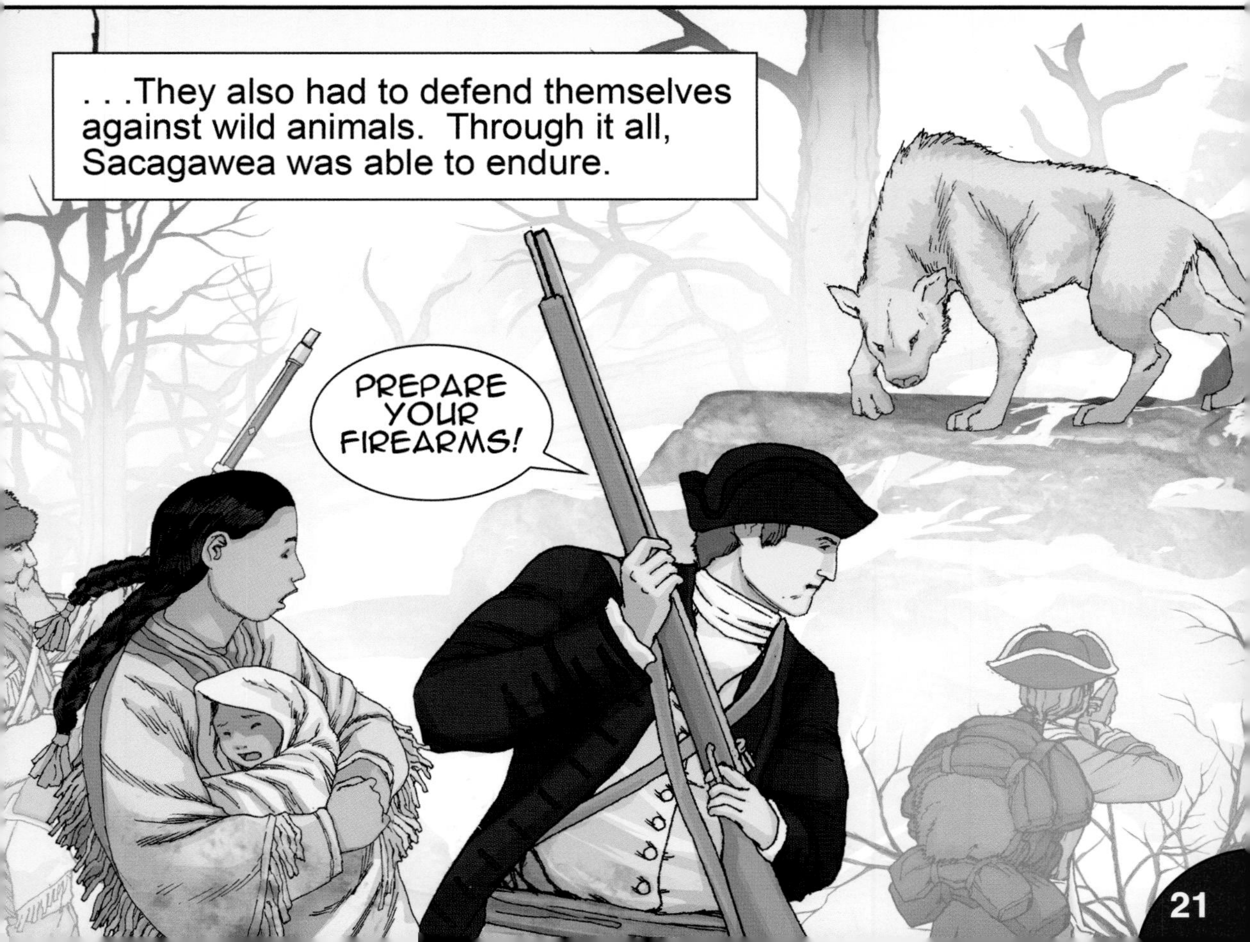
. . .They also had to defend themselves against wild animals. Through it all, Sacagawea was able to endure.
PREPARE YOUR FIREARMS!

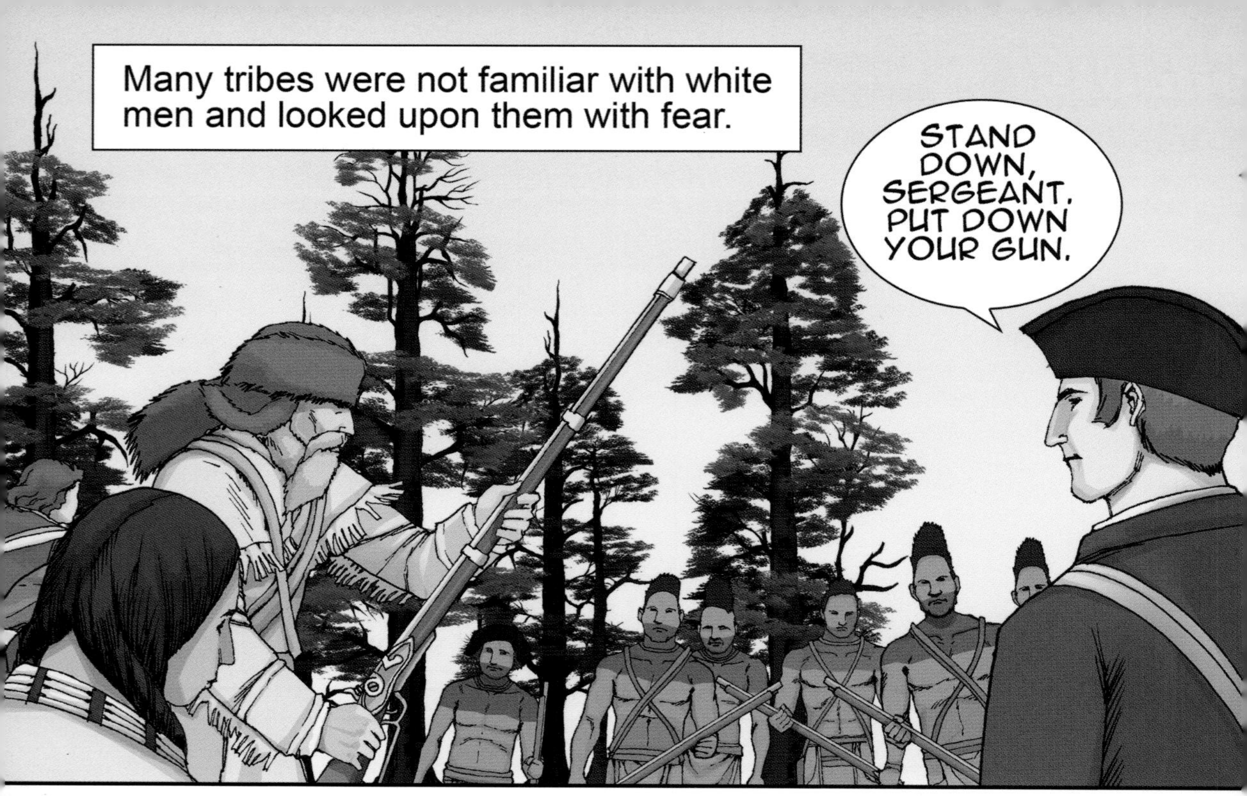
Many tribes were not familiar with white men and looked upon them with fear.
STAND DOWN, SERGEANT. PUT DOWN YOUR GUN.

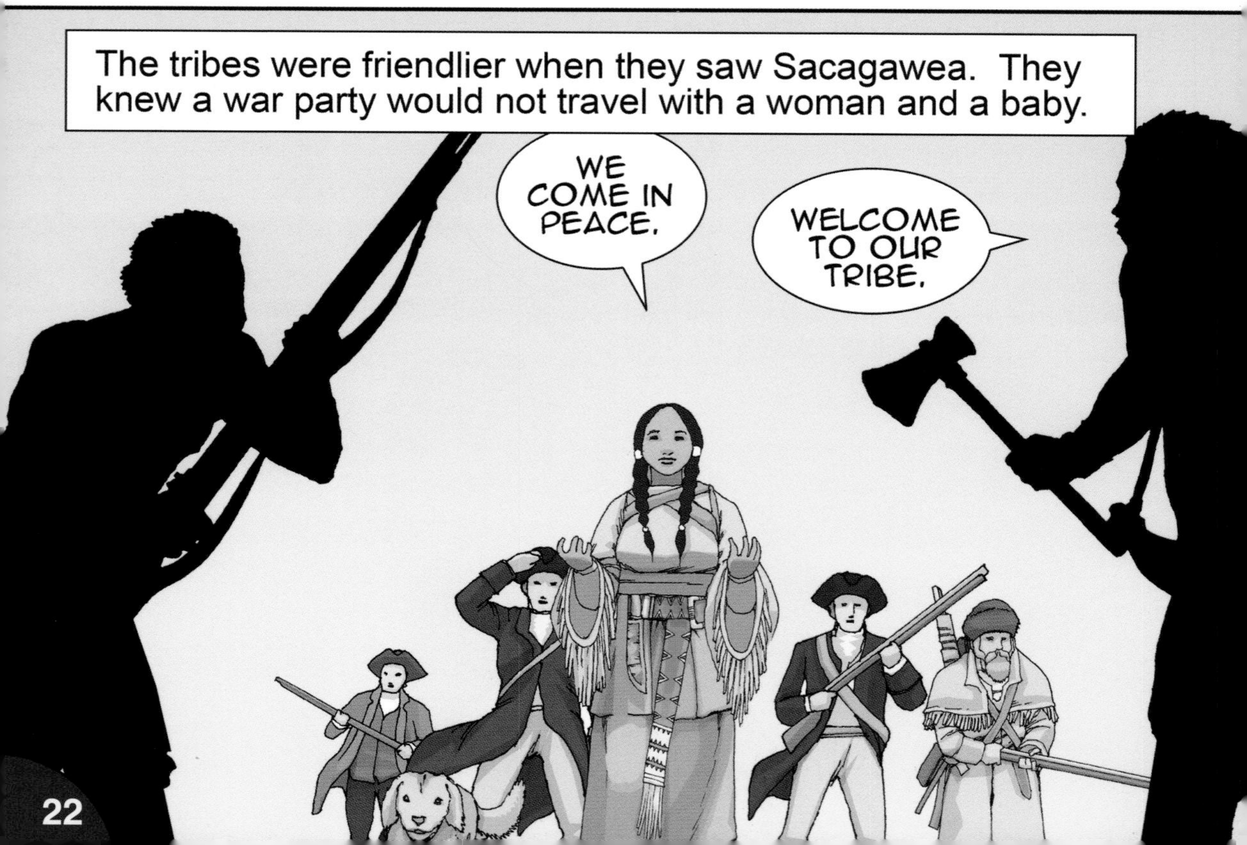
The tribes were friendlier when they saw Sacagawea. They knew a war party would not travel with a woman and a baby.
WE COME IN PEACE.
WELCOME TO OUR TRIBE.

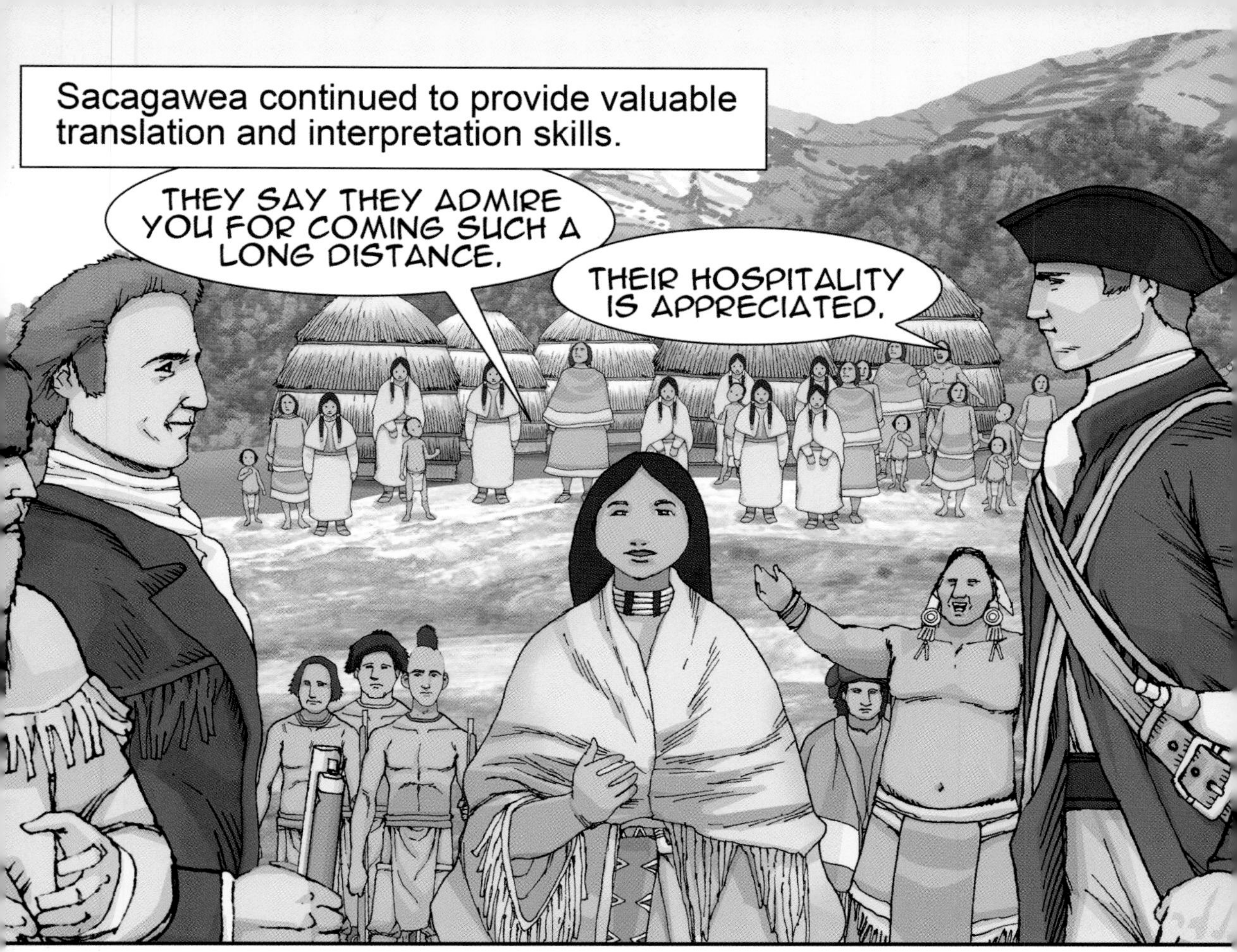
Sacagawea continued to provide valuable translation and interpretation skills.
THEY SAY THEY ADMIRE YOU FOR COMING SUCH A LONG DISTANCE.
THEIR HOSPITALITY IS APPRECIATED.

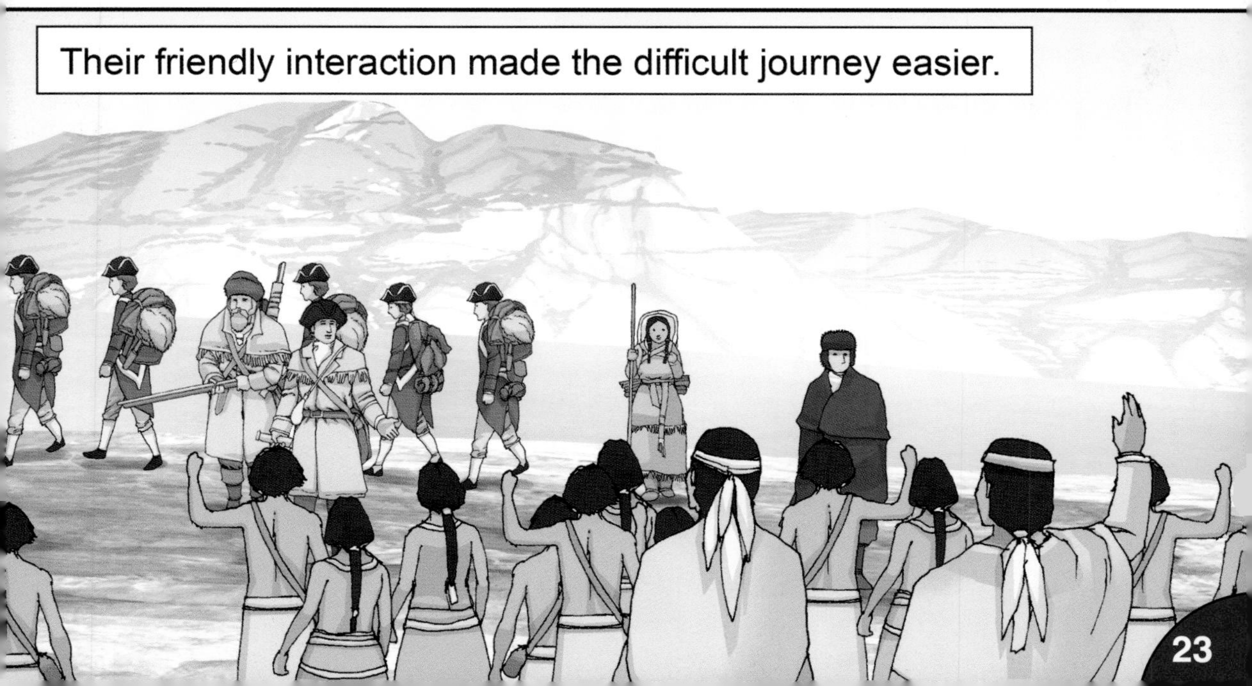
Their friendly interaction made the difficult journey easier.

Chapter 6 The Ocean

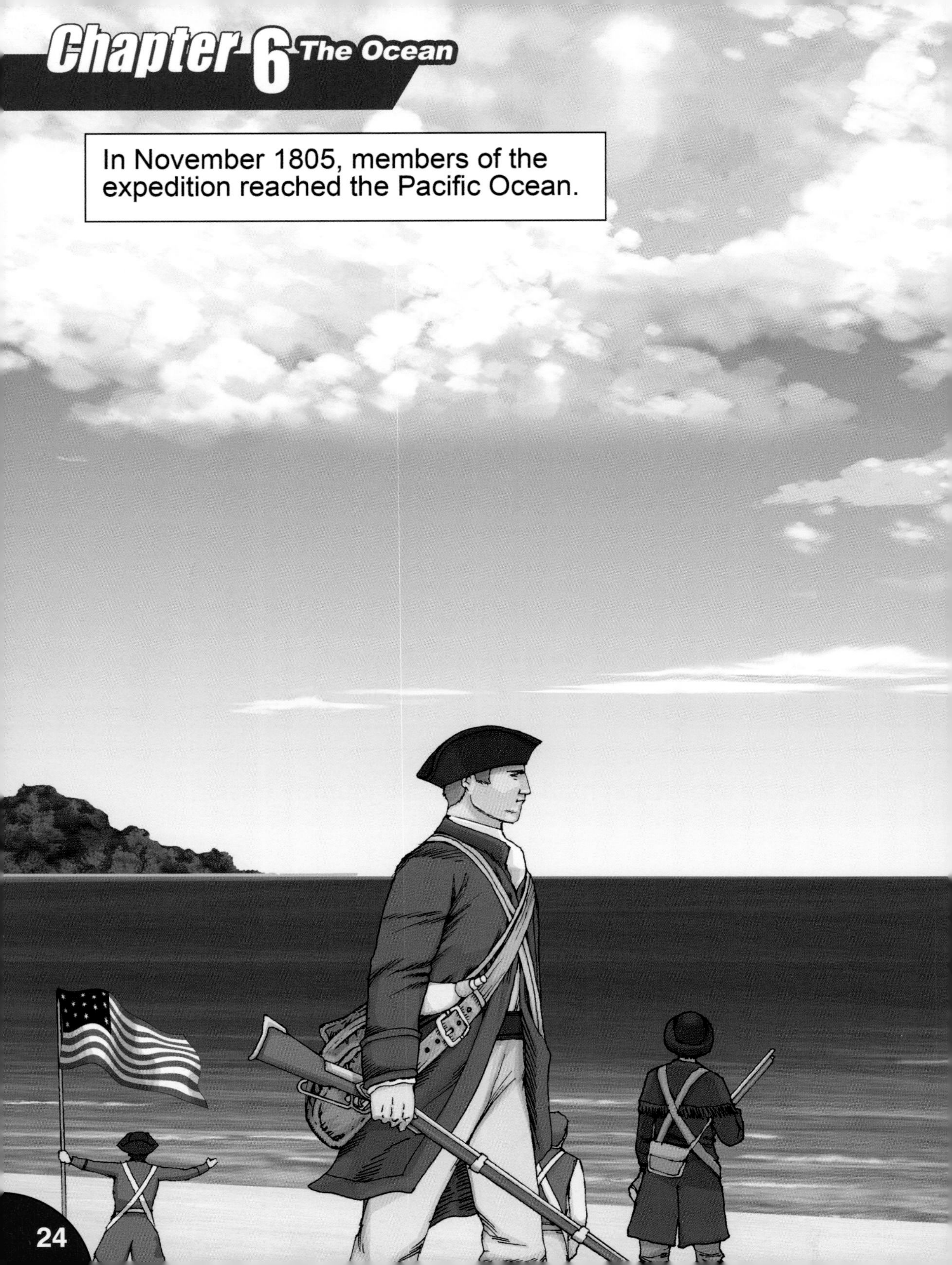
In November 1805, members of the expedition reached the Pacific Ocean.

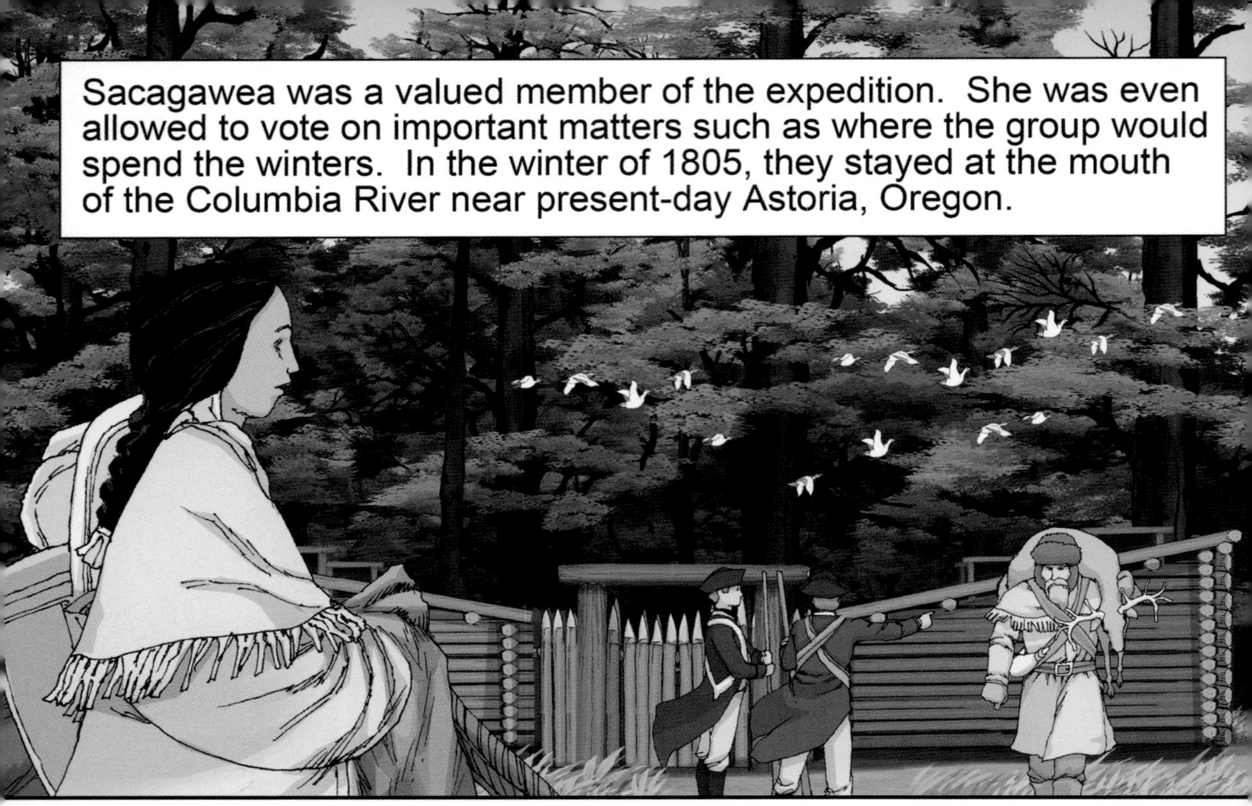
Sacagawea was a valued member of the expedition. She was even allowed to vote on important matters such as where the group would spend the winters. In the winter of 1805, they stayed at the mouth of the Columbia River near present-day Astoria, Oregon.

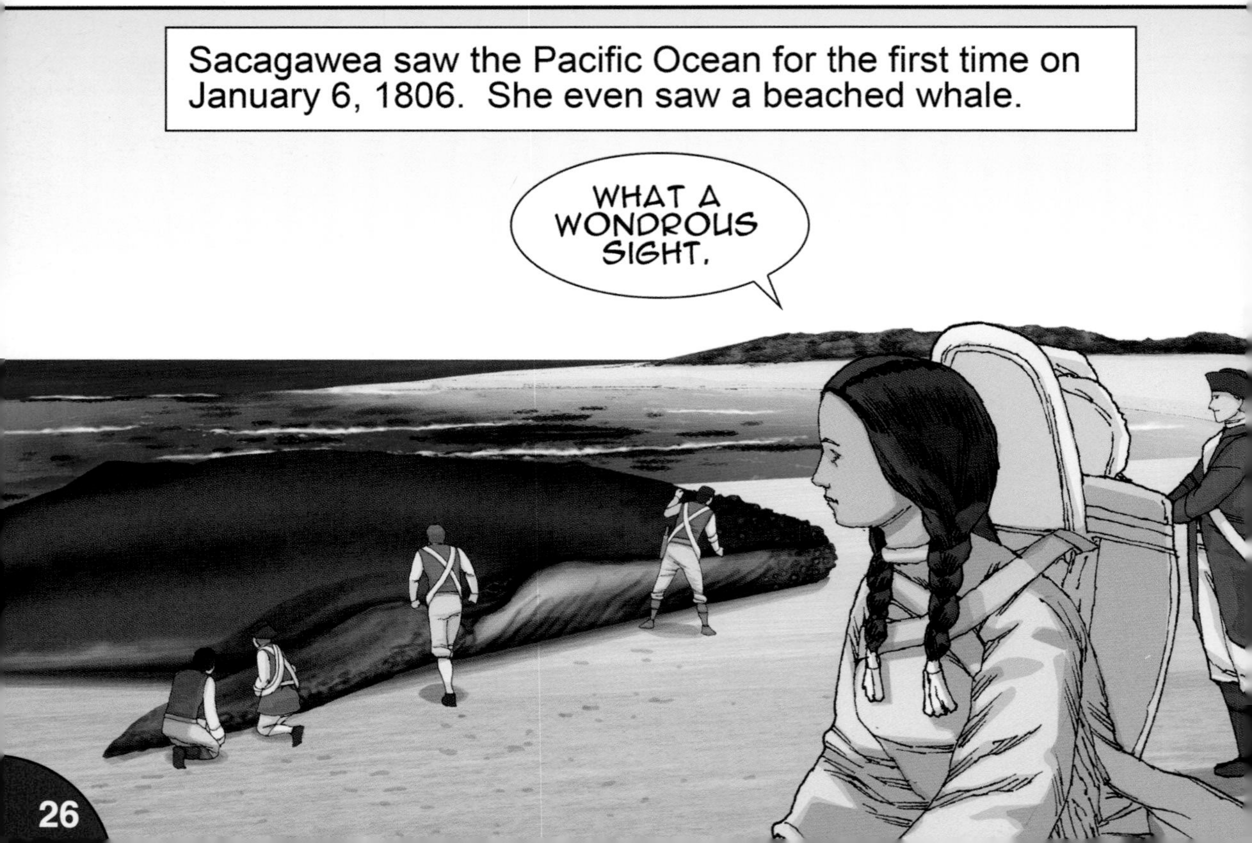
Sacagawea saw the Pacific Ocean for the first time on January 6, 1806. She even saw a beached whale.
WHAT A WONDROUS SIGHT.

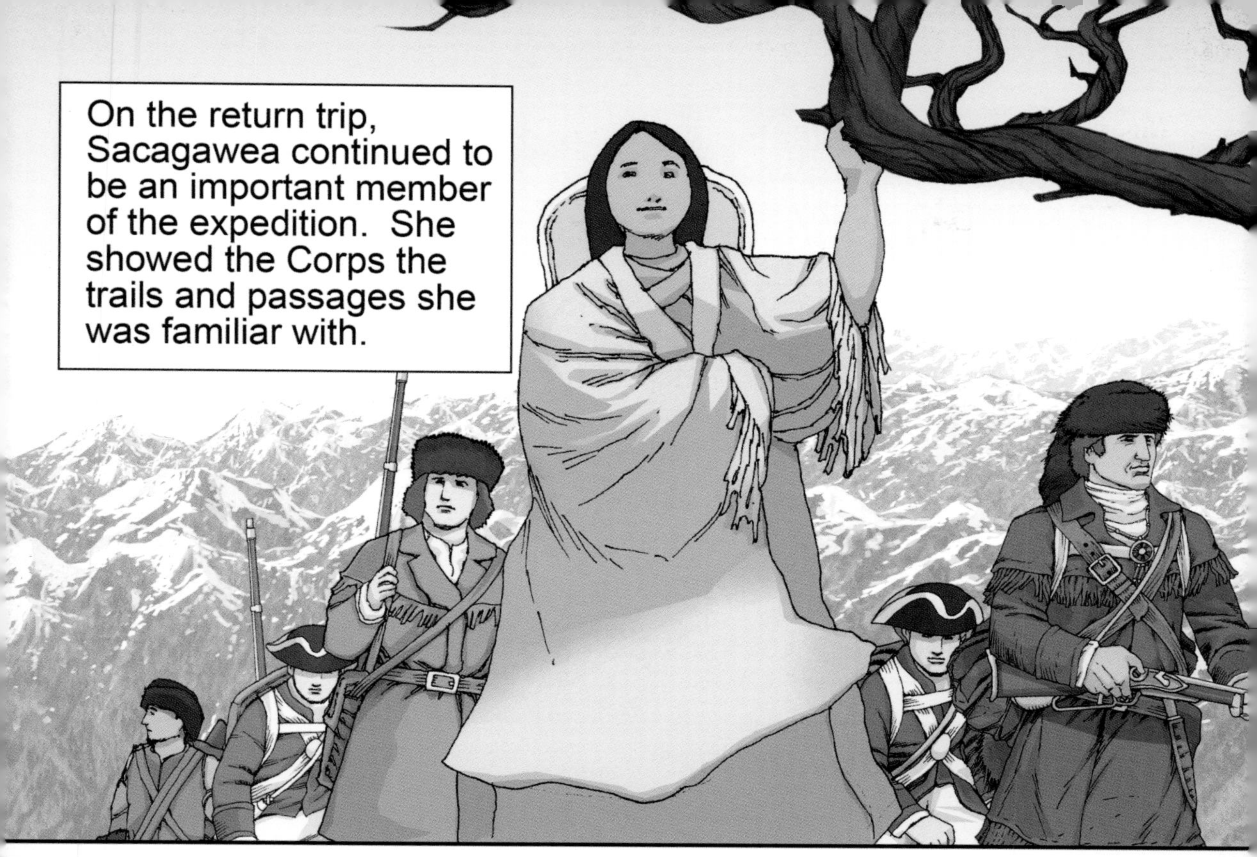
On the return trip, Sacagawea continued to be an important member of the expedition. She showed the Corps the trails and passages she was familiar with.

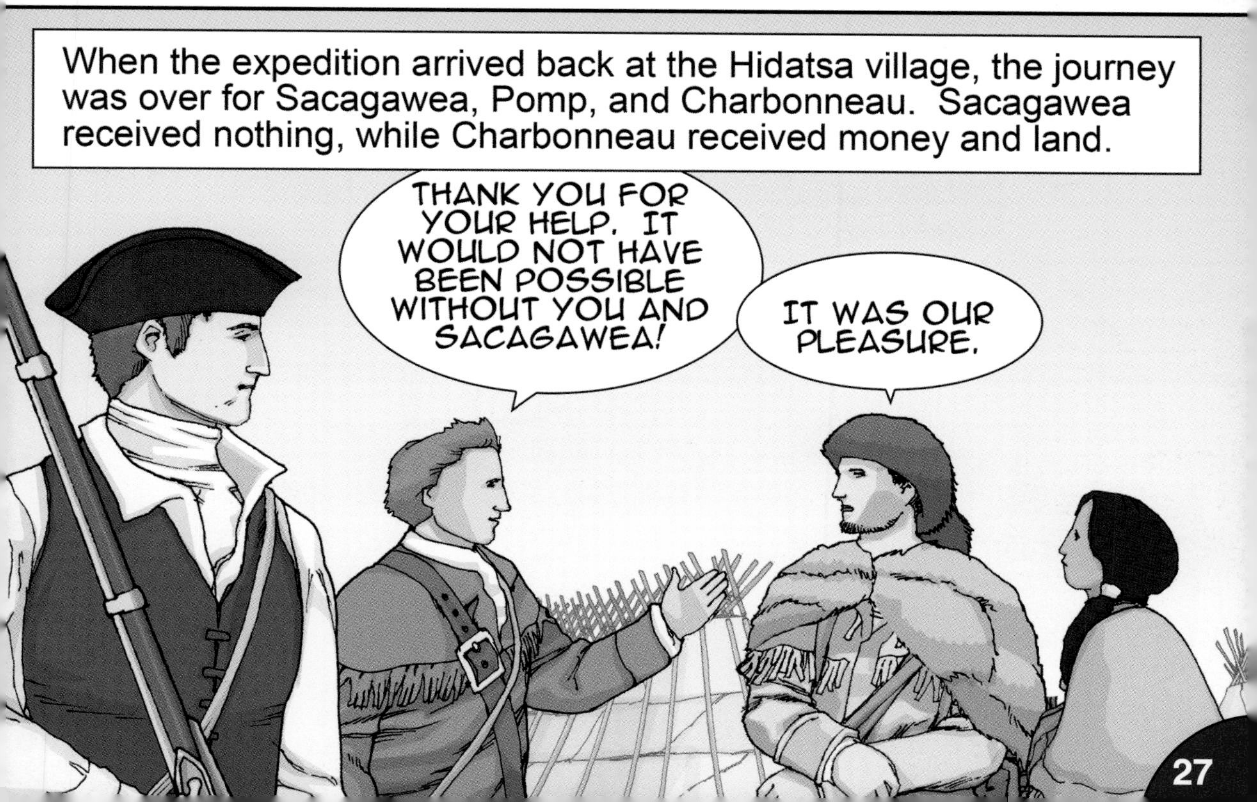
When the expedition arrived back at the Hidatsa village, the journey was over for Sacagawea, Pomp, and Charbonneau. Sacagawea received nothing, while Charbonneau received money and land.
THANK YOU FOR YOUR HELP. IT WOULD NOT HAVE BEEN POSSIBLE WITHOUT YOU AND SACAGAWEA!
IT WAS OUR PLEASURE.

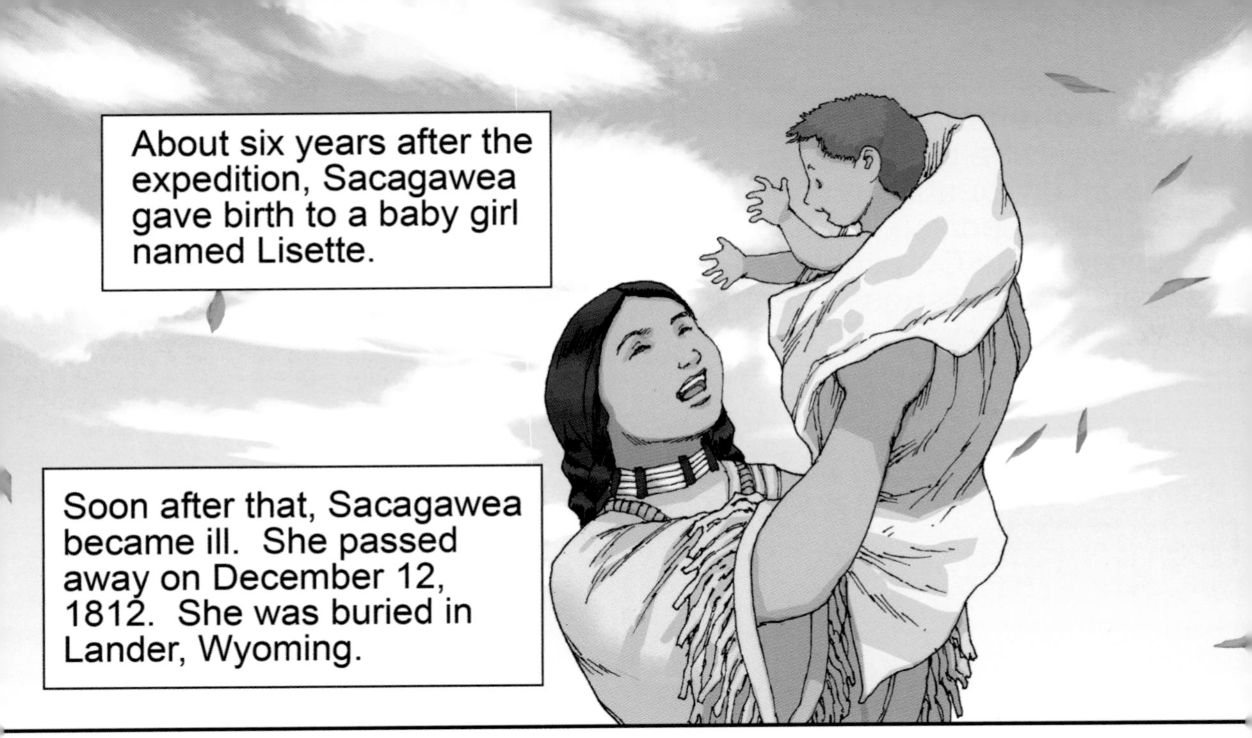
About six years after the expedition, Sacagawea gave birth to a baby girl named Lisette.
Soon after that, Sacagawea became ill. She passed away on December 12, 1812. She was buried in Lander, Wyoming.

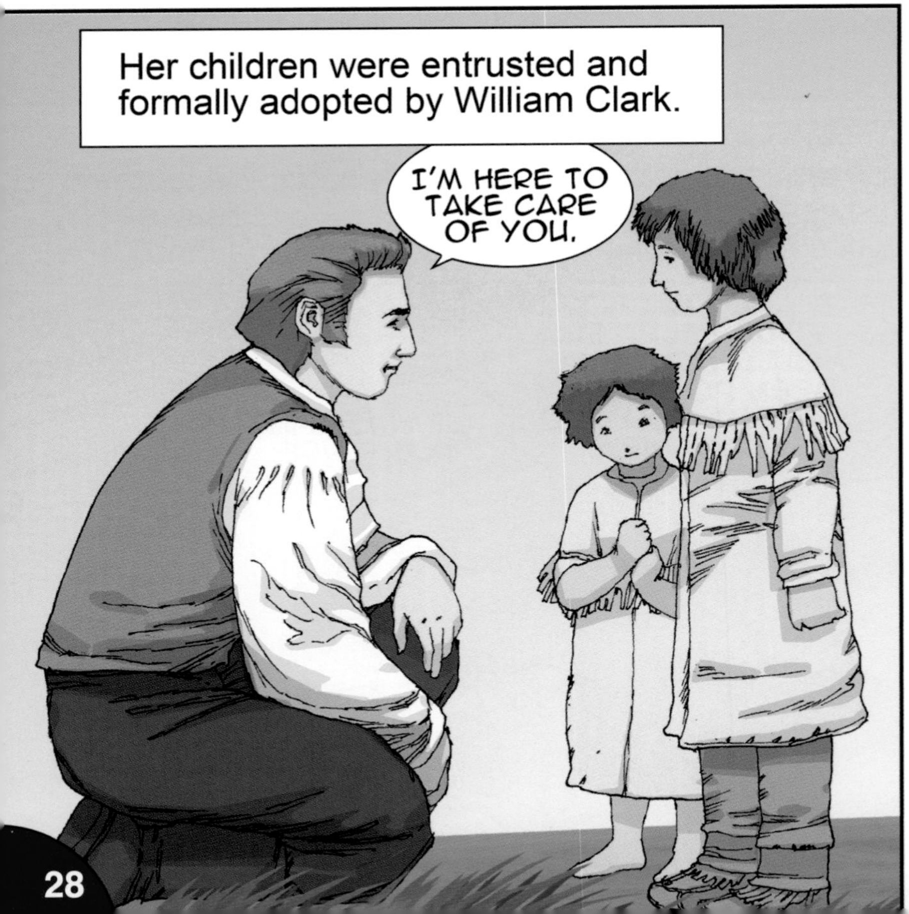
Her children were entrusted and formally adopted by William Clark.
I'M HERE TO TAKE CARE OF YOU.

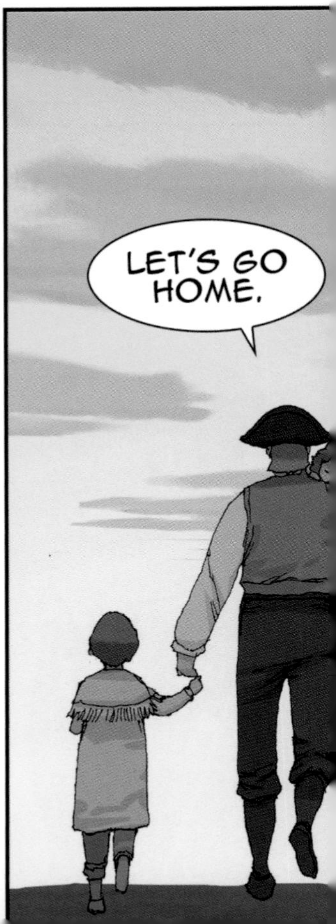
LET'S GO HOME.

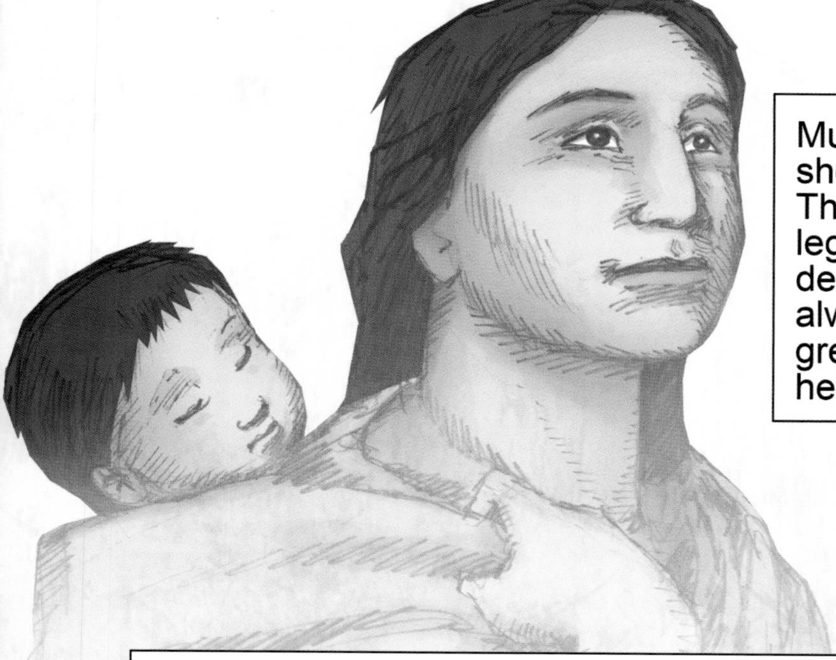

Much of Sacagawea's short life is a mystery. There are many legends about her deeds. But, she will always be known as a great explorer who helped create America.

To honor Sacagawea's contributions, she was recently featured on a U.S. dollar coin. A statue of her also stands in Bismarck, North Dakota. The memory of this legendary explorer will live on forever.

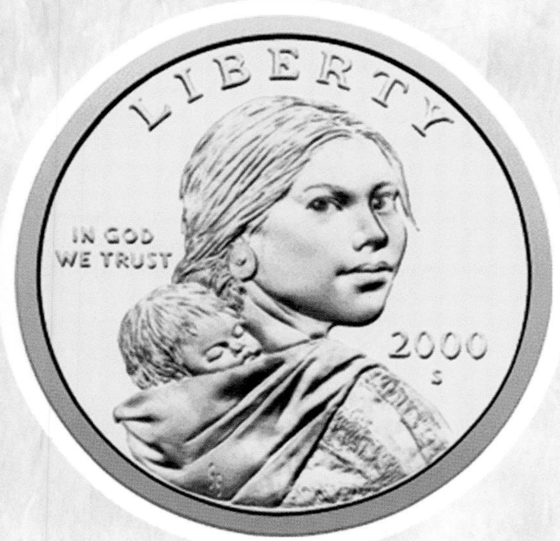
LIBERTY
IN GOD WE TRUST
2000
S

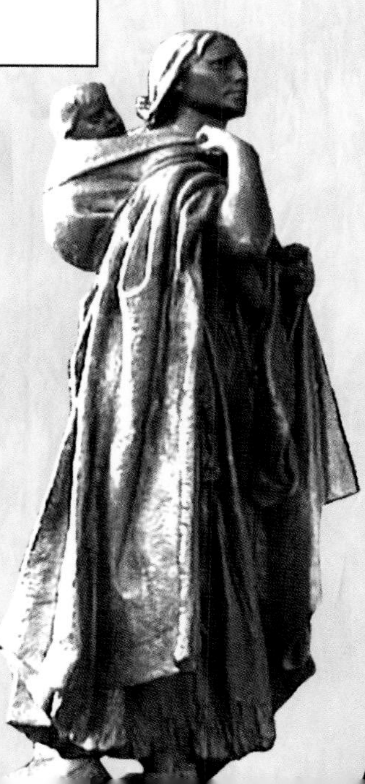

Further Reading

Erdich, Lise. *Sacagawea.* Minneapolis: Lerner Publishing Group, 2005.

Hamilton, John. *Corps of Discovery.* Edina: ABDO Publishing Company, 2003.

Marcovitz, Hal. *Sacagawea: Guide for the Lewis and Clark Expedition.* New York: Facts On File, Inc., 2000.

Petrie, Kristin. *Sacagawea.* Edina: ABDO Publishing Company, 2007.

Columbia River
North Pacific Ocean
Washington
Canoe camp
Traveler's rest
Lewis's return
Maria's River
Ft. Clatsop winter quarters 1805-1806
Great Falls
Clark's return
Ft. Mandan winter quarters 1804-1805
Sacagawea joins the Expedition
Bitterroot Range
Montana
Oregon
Snake River
Idaho
Three Forks camp
Yellowstone River
Missouri River
Mississippi River
Wisconsin
Rocky Mountains
Wyoming
Continental Divide
Sacagawea's Path
Nevada
Nebraska
Platte River
Iowa
Illinois
Utah
Colorado
Missouri River
Departure May 14, 1804
St. Lou
Kansas
California
Missouri
Arizona
New Mexico
Oklahoma
Arkansas
Texas

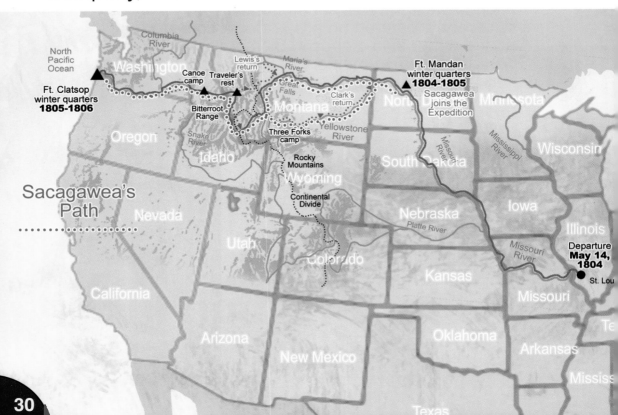

Glossary

capsize - to turn over.

edible - fit to be eaten.

hospitality - having a welcoming and pleasant environment.

kidnap - to carry away by force.

nickname - a descriptive name given to a person by friends, family, or the media.

pristine - not spoiled, corrupted, or polluted.

terrain - the physical features of an area of land. Mountains, rivers, and canyons can all be part of a terrain.

Web Sites

To learn more about Sacagawea, visit ABDO Publishing Company on the World Wide Web at **www.abdopublishing.com.** Web sites about Sacagawea are featured on our Book Links page. These links are routinely monitored and updated to provide the most current information available.

Index